NAPOLEONIC WEAPONS AND WARFARE

NAPOLEONIC
CAVALRY

NAPOLEONIC WEAPONS AND WARFARE

NAPOLEONIC CAVALRY

PHILIP J. HAYTHORNTHWAITE

CASSELL&CO

Cassell & Co
Wellington House, 125 Strand, London WC2R 0BB

First published 2001

British Library Cataloguing-in-Publication data:
A catalogue record for this book is available from
the British Library.

ISBN 0-304-35508-9

Distributed in the USA by Sterling Publishing Co. Inc.,
387 Park Avenue South, New York, NY 10016-8810.

Edited by Michael Boxall.
Additional line illustrations by Terry Hadler.
Design and layout by D.A.G. Publications Ltd., London.

Printed in Great Britain.

CONTENTS

1. INTRODUCTION

2. NAPOLEONIC CAVALRY

3. CAVALRY EQUIPMENT

4. CAVALRY SERVICE

The square was generally impervious to cavalry attack:
British infantry drive off French hussars in the
Peninsula. (Print after H. Dupray.)

INTRODUCTION

WEAPONS AND TACTICS OF THE NAPOLEONIC WARS

In the histories of the Napoleonic Wars, considerable emphasis has been placed upon the skills of the commanding generals. The exercise of those skills, however, was dependent upon the limitations and basic tenets of the prevailing system of 'minor tactics', of the capabilities of the weaponry and the manner whereby these helped determine the way in which armies operated. Each army had its own system of manoeuvre, its own drill and methods of combat, but in the basic principles there was a degree of similarity obvious to all those who participated in the Napoleonic Wars. Such changes as did occur in the methods of combat at the most fundamental level mostly seem to have arisen by evolutionary means rather than by deliberate innovations introduced by the 'great commanders': even Napoleon used a system of war which he found largely in place. The greatest skill, perhaps, lay not with entirely new systems but in the way the accepted ones were utilised and varied at a higher level of tactics.

In this, and the companion volume of *Napoleonic Weapons and Warfare: Infantry*, some consideration is given to these basic factors, the weaponry and how it was used, though it is not intended to list precise specifications of national patterns or to dissect the various drill-books. Indeed, first-hand accounts of what actually happened on the field of battle are often considerably divergent from what the technological specifications of the weaponry and the precise manoeuvre-regulations might suggest should have happened.

Personal accounts of the campaigns were supplemented by discussions on weaponry and tactical methods, many of which occurred in the years following the Napoleonic Wars, in addition to the professional military writings and commentaries produced during the wars. Some degree of circumspection is necessary, however, even with such valuable material, especially if the writer were commenting on something outside his immediate sphere of experience. A member of the British Light Division in the Peninsula made the point: 'We of the infantry are either not informed of all the changes which take place in the rules and regulations for the cavalry, or we do not give them much attention, I fear, if we *are* made acquainted with them. The same observation equally applies with regard to the change of tactics in the infantry. Few cavalry officers, I fancy, give themselves much trouble on that score.'[1] Perhaps this might not be unexpected if George Gleig's comment on the infantry and cavalry were valid, 'the former ... regarding the latter as more ornamental than useful, the latter regarding the former as extremely ungenteel'.[2]

A degree of bias may intrude into otherwise well-reasoned opinions. It was believed at the time that certain nations exhibited particular characteristics, and no matter to what degree it was true, it formed an important part of contemporary military opinion. This was exemplified by the writer who stated that 'we are allowed on all hands to be more able-bodied than the French, and ... individually a far more active and resolute people' as part of his ideas for the improvement of tactical systems. 'Achilles would have been formidable even with the arms of Thersites, but it was only in the Vulcanian arms suited to his strength and power, that the Goddess-born became invulnerable and invincible: it is even thus with British soldiers; they are as formidable as men can be with the present system of

Grenadiers à Cheval of the French Imperial Guard; note the method of carrying the carbine, the butt supported in a leather 'boot'. (Print after 'Caran d'Ache': Emmanuel Poiré.)

tactics, but it is only by a system capable of doing justice to their energy and resolution, that ... their full power of action can be displayed.'[3]

Comments by civilians were viewed askance by some military theorists, exemplified by a criticism of Alison's *History of Europe*: 'When civilians will write military history, and venture to advance opinions of their own on technical points of which the Profession alone are able to judge, they, generally, talk nonsense.'[4] In fairness, it was not just civilians who were guilty: doubts must be raised about some military authors who advanced impracticable theories in the years following the Napoleonic Wars. It was only because of the amount of discussion of tactical matters – at times even heated arguments – that some significant incidents came to be recorded, but so divergent were some of the opinions expressed that anecdotal evidence could be provided to support or counter most theories. Generalisations especially are fraught with hazard, because evidence to support or counter any particular theory might actually involve a singular incident involving peculiar circumstances unlikely to be repeated elsewhere. Misconceptions were not unknown – neither at the time, nor in later commentaries.

Some contemporary opinions were justified by reference to the experiences of past generations, and even to classical antiquity. These might not have been relevant to the warfare of the time, and as one Austrian commentator remarked, reading the wrong things, or not appreciating the difference between ancient and modern warfare, could be counter-productive. (He added that it was not necessary for a subaltern to learn anything of the higher tenets of ancient strategy, as he would be unlikely ever to command a large body of troops.) It was also possible to form an unbalanced view by using only a limited number of sources. Many of the references to 'minor tactics' were written by British commentators, perhaps because the relatively smaller scale of their actions (when compared to the great battles of continental Europe and the larger formations employed) tended to throw the emphasis of their writing upon the performance of small units, rather than the 'grand tactics' which concerned many of the others.

Understanding of the tactics and experiences of the Napoleonic Wars must be founded upon the published drill- and manoeuvre-regulations employed by every army; but the degree to which these dictated events on the battlefield is debatable. Accounts exist of units following precise parade-ground drill under fire, but alternatively of units more resembling the actions of a confused mob, and there is perhaps some justification for the comment by one veteran that 'the argument of what *might* have happened, but which *did not* happen, is like entering into that complicated point, that if your aunt was not your aunt, she might have been your uncle'.5 Furthermore, contemporary accounts may be distorted by the writer's lack of appreciation of how the enemy was *intended* to operate, hence one description of a French deployment adopting the straggling and haphazard manner characteristic of that army, when the troops in question were doubtless both well-disciplined and experienced.

The importance of the principle of military training cannot be under-estimated. Only by drilling troops until some manoeuvres and formations became automatic could some degree of order be retained on the battlefield, where operations had to be conducted under conditions of confusion, noise, bad visibility and terror. Knowledge of what a soldier was supposed to do in combat, ingrained upon the parade-ground, and the confidence that his fellows also knew what to do, was essential for the maintenance of morale, and it was morale which held units together in circumstances of unimaginable horror when the day of trial came; as one writer remarked, 'An "extra grain of pluck" is, after all, no more than sufficiency of confidence' which came from understanding the drill.6

The French Marshal Auguste Marmont stated that native courage was not of much significance until allied to organisation, discipline ('to accustom inferiors to a blind obedience towards their superiors') and tactical instruction, which

Austrian hussar trooper, c. 1798–1806. The sabre is hung from the wrist by the sword-knot, while the carbine is used; its ramrod is attached to the shoulder-belt by means of a leather strap. (Print after R. von Ottenfeld.)

together produced mutual confidence among the soldiers and confidence in their commanders, without which an army lost half its value.

Calculations could be made about the smallest aspects of drill, for example, of how long it took respective armies to form line from column; but there must be a suspicion that such meticulous precision is somewhat irrelevant when battlefield conditions are considered, if only because the terrain was hardly likely to be as easy to traverse as the parade-ground on which the 'regulation' statistics could be calculated. At times there must have been such confusion in combat that only an approximation of the regulation drill can have been put into practice; and to imagine, because men had been trained to load and fire like automata irrespective of the carnage and confusion around them, that units would invariably manoeuvre in battle as they would on the parade-ground is surely to over-estimate the effect of drilling. This seems to have been appreciated at the time, and in some cases the official regulations were probably regarded as a basis for discipline, manoeuvre and morale-building rather than an inviolable guide to what occurred on the battlefield. Equally, it would be wrong to ignore the contribution that drill could make; to regard it all as 'complicated manoeuvres ... which, like Chinese puzzles, only engross time and labour to the unprofitable end of forming useless combinations',[7] as Ludlow Beamish commented on part of the cavalry drill, would be equally misleading. Indeed, the need to appreciate a number of general principles would seem to be the only explanation of how units could, in the heat of battle, perform basic manoeuvres and adopt formations which may never have been rehearsed and were certainly not part of the established regulations, as seems to have happened at times.

The Duke of Wellington recognised that proficiency at drill was not sufficient to create a proficient army: 'Those take an erroneous view of what an army is, if they suppose that well-drilled recruits are all that is required for it. Subordination and habits of obedience are more necessary than mechanical discipline acquired at the drill; and these can be acquired by soldiers to any useful purpose only in proportion as they have confidence in their officers ... the object of all drill must be to practice and form individuals to perform that which it is thought expedient they should perform when part of a body before an enemy.' Commenting on what he regarded as the folly of sending well-drilled men to Spanish regiments not so proficient he stated that under such circumstances, 'the well drilled recruit is no better than the rabble with whom he is mixed up; and he either very soon forgets all that he has learnt for want of practice, or despises it as useless, as he finds that the boasters among whom he comes have none of the acquirements which he has gained with so much trouble; or he despises the ignorance of his officers and comrades, and has no confidence in either, or in himself'.[8]

The idea that the only instruction really necessary was that to enable troops to perform adequately 'before an enemy' was echoed by other commentators, like the Austrian who averred that on the day of battle the soldier should concentrate upon only two things: feeling with his elbows those of the men next to him, and neither preceding them, nor allowing them to precede him. In fact, some troops seem to have been pushed into action in time of emergency with not much more instruction than that: in 1813, for example, the French General Jean-Baptiste Girard reported that his division knew how to form square from column and vice versa, but little else. Others might not be conversant with the drill-manuals for different reasons; for example, Wellington's complaint about the perception of regulations: 'If discipline means habits of obedience to orders, as well as military instruction, we have but little of it in the army. Nobody ever thinks of obeying an order; and all regulations ... are so much waste paper.' (Even so, he added, 'It is, however, an unrivalled army for fighting, if the soldiers can only be kept in their ranks during the battle.'[9])

That the drill-regulations might not be easy to comprehend is another factor. A story was told of Colonel Francis Skelly Tidy, who commanded the British 3/14th Foot at Waterloo and the 44th in Burma, when discussing a set of manoeuvre-regulations subsequent to those used during the Napoleonic Wars: it was remarked to him that 'the learned work of Sir H. Torrens had been translated into Burmese, and might do mischief, as giving them an insight into European tactics. "Oh!" said Tidy, "there is no fear of that. We cannot understand it in English, still less will the Burmese be able to make anything of it."'[10]

A British officer wrote of a factor probably universal in all armies: 'When officers from home came out to us, we found them too frequently impregnated with all the punctilios enforced by the Horse Guards clock; with ideas redolent of hair-powder and blank cartridge; stiff in stocks, starched in frills, with Dundas's eighteen manoeuvres or commandments. All this had to be changed ... at length they began to discover how the art was carried on, and found that they had much to unlearn, as well as much to acquire, before they could make themselves useful.'[11]

That even the most carefully instilled drill might break down, or be found impracticable, under the stresses of the battlefield would not seem to be in doubt. A classic story which demonstrates the point concerns Sir David Dundas, alias 'Old Pivot' (from the 'pivots' employed in his Prussian-inspired and very influential drill-book used by the British Army). On one occasion in the Netherlands in 1794–5 even his own brigade fell into great disorder, whereupon a friend and fellow-countryman rode up and asked mischievously,'I say, David, whar's your peevots noo?'[12] Many of the actual occurrences on the battlefield may have been the result of practical experience rather than book-learning, and indeed some veterans implied that even some fundamentals were not covered by the drill-manuals; from retrospective remarks by veterans, for example, there must be a suspicion that even the French 1791 manual was less respected in practice than some commentators suggested. As late as 1845 it was observed of British officers that 'they generally depend for their tactical learning upon the instruction communicated orally in the drill-field. The book of Regulations is seldom opened, except, perhaps, to settle some disputed point of minute detail.' The writer recalled a commanding officer who told his officers: 'Gentlemen, the General intends to look at the regiment tomorrow. He desires me to say that he will require some light movements, and that he wishes you in the meanwhile to look at the book, which of course you will do ... not that, for my part, I see anything in books or theory.'[13]

Those forces – generally irregulars – who *had* no regulations by which to be guided should also be

The Guard: a version of the illustration which demonstrated the movement in the British 1796 Rules and Regulations for the Sword Exercise of Cavalry.

taken into consideration. Troops of this nature were by no means inevitably ineffective, especially in conditions conducive to their mode of operation: Cossacks and guerrillas in Spain and the Tyrol are obvious examples.

When all such factors are considered, the importance of the evidence of eyewitness accounts becomes clear, to demonstrate examples of what actually happened rather than what should have happened according to the official manuals.

Officer of French Chevau-Légers-Lanciers. This print after Martinet must date from 1814, for the royal emblem of a fleur-de-lys has been painted on to the plate on the pouch-belt.

Two further factors should be considered when assessing the performance of weaponry and the impact it had upon methods of military operations. Despite developments in weapon-technology and tactics, there must be much truth in the remark of the later French commentator, Colonel C. J. J. J. Ardant du Picq, who stated that the one unchangeable aspect was the heart of men, and that in the final analysis it was morale which was the deciding factor (although, however accurate that may be, the capability of the weaponry and the manner in which it was used must have been considerable factors in the maintenance or decline of morale).

Finally, when considering the techniques of warfare and capability of the weaponry, it should never be overlooked that the net result was the visitation of mutilation and death upon countless thousands. Many writers who were witness to such havoc left moving accounts of its results, such as the following description of the field of Borodino on the evening of the battle, which:

was awful and bloody in the extreme; the massacre on both sides was without a parallel in the history of modern warfare.

Both armies fought with desperate bravery ... we fought to conquer, they to defend their country; and they did it bravely... our oldest troopers, who from 1792 had traversed Europe sword in hand, and fought in Italy, Germany, Austria, and Egypt, under Moreau, Jourdan, Dumourier, and Bonaparte, had seen nothing in their whole career to equal the dreadful picture before them on the evening of the memorable 6th of September, 1812. As to myself, I was horror-struck, and half frantic, from beholding so many brave fellows writhing in the agonies of a protracted death, and hearing their heart-rending moans; strewed around me in heaps, like one confused mass of human misery ... the earth was literally concealed by one mass of the bodies of men and horses, helmets and uniforms saturated in blood. Amid these positions, what ample scenes for contemplation and remorse presented themselves! An immense plain, as far as the eye could reach, was literally strewed with men, many of whom were yet struggling in death. Occasionally from amid this awful cemetery a dark and ghastly head would be raised, besmeared with blood and gunpowder, while the suffering and half-frantic men called out vainly for assistance!

The writer also made a comment the content of which was repeated in many accounts by witnesses of similar horror and futility:

Would that some vaunting utopians and conquerors could behold such scenes of misery and death, when they would uphold by the sword some wild doctrine or principle. Such a scene might suggest to them more peaceful, certainly more humane measures. But to such men, alas! of what avail the lives of thousands, the happiness of millions, or the ruin or prosperity of states? They are bigoted to a principle. They must conquer: not by the dictates of wisdom or humanity, but by the physical force of arms; to win which one-half of their subjects must be immolated – and this is their triumph.[14]

* * * * *

In this text it has been thought practical to provide source-footnotes only to direct quotations. To facilitate further study, English-language sources or English translations are quoted whenever possible.

French cuirassiers charge into the Raevsky Redoubt at Borodino. (Print after Albrecht Adam).

NAPOLEONIC CAVALRY

COMPOSITION AND DUTIES

One of the three principal elements of an army, the cavalry was generally divided into light and heavy regiments, each with its own function, though some, described at times as 'medium' cavalry, have been considered as an intermediate stage between the two. In many cases, however, the actual situation seems not to have been quite so conveniently divided.

It was usually stated that the duty of the light regiments was to provide the army with its reconnaissance facility, forming a highly mobile and fast-moving force which could not only scout, precede an advance or cover a retreat, but also provide the army's security by maintaining a chain of posts to shield it from enemy reconnaissance and surprise attacks; and to be able to raid and harass the enemy. The heavy regiments, conversely, were held to be best suited for action on the battlefield, to execute massed charges upon the enemy, ideally against a weakened section of his line; to make a breakthrough and enable the light regiments to conduct the pursuit once the enemy had been beaten. Consequently, the larger mounts were usually allocated to the heavy regiments, the smaller and swifter mounts to the light regiments, but in practice the distinctions were not always so clearly defined. Although in larger forces the cavalry might be sufficient in numbers for the heavy regiments to be concentrated for use in 'shock' action, in armies with less cavalry the available mounted troops might have to fulfil whatever role was needed, without the luxury of being able to allocate particular units to a specific duty. Writers accustomed to serving with this more universal type of cavalry might be expected to be more critical than others of the different types maintained by other armies; for example, one British commentator described the heavy cavalry of some Germanic armies as 'clumsily accoutred' and mounted upon the sort of horse otherwise only to be found pulling the drays of Barclay & Perkins (a well-known British brewer!) Another remarked that cavalry 'must be mounted on horses fully equal to the weight they have to carry ... heavy cavalry and heavy infantry are terms for heavy heads to amuse themselves with ... cavalry and infantry, if they are to be strong, must be light also'.[15] Wellington, for example, was among those who deplored the attempt to create within the small British Army all the types of cavalry which could be maintained by larger armies: 'We form five descriptions of cavalry ... as many descriptions, as far as dress and ornament may go, as any other army whatever possesses; and the consequence is, we have nothing perfect.' He advocated the alternative view that *all* cavalry should be capable of doing whatever was required, 'be they dressed or armed as they may'.[16]

Despite such opinions, the distinction between heavy and light regiments was generally maintained. The heaviest cavalry of all were those styled cuirassiers (from the cuirass or armour for the body), though not all those bearing the name actually wore armour: the Russian cuirassier regiments only adopted it in 1813–14, and the Prussian cuirassiers in 1814, for example. Most famous were those in Napoleon's army, which he converted in 1802–3 from the existing heavy regiments (that had been merely styled *Cavalerie*), augmented by the two Carabinier regiments, which received armour from 1808. The issue of the cuirass was a sign of the use Napoleon intended to make of them, exclusively as a striking-force on the battlefield, and unsuited for other tasks. Wellington described Napoleon's employment of cuirassiers as 'a kind of accelerated infantry',[17] capable of overpowering the enemy and capturing ground, instead of an arm which supported and exploited the efforts of others. The French cuirassiers attained a reputation which intimidated their opponents, from the 'shock' effect of armoured men on large horses, as well as from their courage: one of their officers, Aymar de Gonneville, recalled how in 1807 he charged a body of Prussian hussars who seemed inclined to meet them, having mistaken the French (from their helmets) for dragoons; but when they drew their swords, throwing back their cloaks and

Left: *Standards or guidons were issued to many cavalry regiments, squadrons or even troops, but were carried in action only comparatively rarely. This contemporary drawing depicts that of the New Romney Fencible Cavalry.*

Right: *The evolution of a typical heavy cavalry uniform, as worn by French Gendarmerie; left to right: 1700–50; 1789–1804; 1810 (Gendarmerie d'Espagne); 1810 (Gendarmerie d'Elite); 1815–30; 1841. (Print after Charles Vernier.)*

Left: *French heavy cavalry, c. 1795, showing the method of carrying the carbine butt-downwards, in a leather 'boot' attached to the saddle. (Engraving by Quichon after Hippolyte Bellangé.)*

revealing their cuirasses, the hussars began to waver and were thus overthrown by the charge. Heavy regiments in other armies bore a number of designations, from Garde du Corps to Dragoon Guards (in the British army) and Dragoons.

Dragoons are sometimes described as 'medium' cavalry, midway between the heavy and light regiments, though this was a classification rarely given at the time. The origin of such troops, in the seventeenth century, was as mounted infantry, armed with muskets, who could ride into battle and then fight on foot (their name being derived from their firearm). By the Napoleonic era, however, this role had been lost; dragoons were generally regarded as heavy cavalry, but unlike the heaviest also able to perform some of the duties of the lighter regiments. The last use of dragoons in a way resembling the old style was Napoleon's creation of *Dragons à Pied* ('foot dragoons') which served most notably in 1806, but the plan was not a great success and differed from the original concept in that they were employed as ordinary infantry, not infantry that rode into battle. The flexibility of the French dragoons was demonstrated in the later campaigns, when they formed the backbone of Napoleon's mounted arm. In northern and eastern Europe they were employed as heavy cavalry – especially valuable after the losses of 1812 and the subsequent difficulties in procuring the larger horses required by the cuirassiers – while those in the Iberian peninsula fulfilled in addition the role of lighter cavalry, for example in anti-guerrilla operations.

Marmont envisaged a quite different role for dragoons. He advocated that there should be three types of cavalry, with specific functions: light regiments to reconnoitre and provide intelligence of the enemy; line regiments to engage the enemy cavalry and pursue a defeated opponent; and armoured line regiments to engage the enemy infantry. Dragoons, he thought, should be returned to their original function of mounted infantry, riding horses too small for the line cavalry so as to prevent their commanders from using them as proper cavalry (which, of course, they actually were during the Napoleonic Wars). A number of armies maintained units of Mounted Riflemen (commonly styled *Jäger zu Pferd* as they were usually German), and Prussian cavalry regiments in the period of the 'War of Liberation' (1813–14) had detachments of *Freiwilligen Jäger* ('volunteer Jägers') attached to them, but these provided an enhanced skirmish capability rather than being mounted infantry in the original sense of the term envisaged by Marmont. The nearest that any Napoleonic formation came to the original concept of dragoons was probably the French *Régiment des Dromadaires* or camel corps, formed during the Egyptian expedition, which used camels for movement but dismounted to fight.

Above: Austrian cuirassiers, wearing the 1798 helmet. (Print after R. von Ottenfeld.)

The light regiments included the large body styled *Chasseurs à Cheval* or their equivalent (such as the German term *Chevauxlegers*, from the French *Chevau-Légers*, 'light horse'), and the British Light Dragoons. Two further categories existed in many armies: hussars and lancers. The former were copied from the Hungarian light horse which had proved so effective in Imperial (Austrian) service, renowned especially for bravery and *élan*, and in emulation of these troops, most armies equipped their hussars with a uniform which owed its origin to the Hungarian style, notably the pelisse,

Right: Unless in square, infantry were very vulnerable to attack by cavalry: French dragoons ride into British infantry at Alexandria. (Print after H. Dupray.)

Below: French Dragons à Pied skirmishing, still retaining their cavalry sabres even though serving as infantry. (Print after Horace Vernet.)

dolman, fur cap and sabretache. In many cases this was accompanied by a swaggering attitude exemplified by a remark of Antoine Lasalle, the archetypal French hussar, who declared that any hussar not dead by the age of thirty was a blackguard (he was killed at Wagram, aged thirty-four). Some commentators criticised the nature of hussar uniform, 'the tiddy dol appearance ... the fribbling ornaments with which they are attired would better become an equestrian performer on one of our inferior stages, than a hardy veteran, when equipped for the field',[18] although it doubtless contributed to the *esprit de corps* of such troops. Another, with much truth, remarked that it was not the pelisse and dolman which made a hussar, but the man inside, and that the skill, *élan* and physical qualities of the Hungarians made them the only *true* hussars. In a similar manner, a number of armies formed units of lancers, based upon the traditional Polish light horse, and often dressed in Polish-style uniforms; they are considered below in the section on lances.

The French hussar, Albert de Rocca, explained the character of the light cavalry as a product of the duties they undertook in the field:

> The hussars and chasseurs were generally accused of being plunderers and prodigal, loving drink and fancying everything fair while in the presence of the enemy. Accustomed, one may say, to sleep with an open eye, to have an ear always awake to the sound of the trumpet, to reconnoitre far in advance during a march, to trace the ambuscades of the enemy, to observe the slightest traces of their marches, to examine defiles, and to scan the plains with eagle sight, they could not fail to have acquired superior intelligence and habits of independence ... the light horseman, under his large cloak, braved in every country the rigour of the season. The rider and his horse, accustomed to live together, contracted a character of resemblance. The rider derived animation from his horse, and the horse from his rider ...[19]

Officer of the 1st (Polish) Chevau-Légers (left) and trooper of the Dragoons (right) of the French Imperial Guard. The dragoon wears his waist-belt lengthened to form a second shoulder-belt. (Print by Lacoste after Eugène Lami.).

Most armies allocated horses according to the type of cavalryman to be mounted upon them, though the distinction between light and heavy cavalry was not always maintained, especially in wartime when there was often difficulty in procuring suitable remounts. The largest and strongest horses were normally allocated to the heaviest regiments; in French service in 1812, for example, horses of 15 hands were regarded as the largest mounts for *chasseurs* and hussars, the smallest for dragoons; 15.3 hands the largest for dragoons but the smallest for cuirassiers and carabiniers, with the smallest

An archetypal hussar and one of the best commanders of light cavalry during the period: Antoine-Charles-Louis, comte de Lasalle (1775–1809), killed at Wagram. (Print after François Flameng.)

horses of all, 14.3 to 14.7 hands, being reserved for the *Chevau-Légers* (horses for the equivalent formations in the Imperial Guard were slightly bigger than those for the line).

At times such statistics were somewhat notional, as the rigours of campaigning resulted in the use of many horses smaller than the regulations intended. Faber du Faur's well-known picture of a French cuirassier and carabinier mounted upon grotesquely undersized Russian ponies during the 1812 campaign may be an extreme, but it was a constant problem. Even in the British Army, sometimes stated to have had the best horses (if not always the best cared-for, excluding the King's German Legion cavalrymen who were renowned for putting the comfort of their mounts before their own), it was possible for a light dragoon officer to complain in 1809 that his regiment had received a draft of virtual 'cart horses' from the Irish Commissariat, which had already been rejected in England as unsuitable for heavy dragoons, but which had been sent instead to a light regiment which needed the swiftest, most agile mounts. In some cases the difference between the mounts of light and heavy cavalry may not have been very marked. In 1813, for example, the average size of the horses of the British 10th Hussars was about 15 hands, those of the heavier 2nd Dragoons 15.2 hands, with the latter having about eight per cent of their horses only $14\frac{1}{2}$ hands.

There are many recorded comments to the effect that the heavier horses were simply not capable of performing the duties required of light cavalry, but conversely that in battle the heavier horses enjoyed a distinct advantage. For example, Captain William Hay of the British 12th Light Dragoons recalled that his regiment's horses were considerably lighter than those of the French *light* cavalry they encountered at Waterloo, but on witnessing the charge of the Union Brigade noted that 'notwithstanding my experience as a cavalry officer [I never] considered what a great difference there was in a charge of a light and a heavy dragoon regiment, from the weight and power of the horses and men'.[20] There were examples of light horse upsetting heavy, however, although (as in the case of the victory of Austrian hussars over French carabiniers at Leipzig, for example) this may have depended less upon the size of mount as upon the morale of the troops involved. Regarding the latter, there was probably a deal of truth in the remark made by one commentator to the effect that 'We have never witnessed any charge in which the weight seemed to have much to do with the matter, nor do we think it has, *always supposing that the dragoon has a sufficient horse under him*, and feels confident that his steed can *carry him well into the fray and safely out of it.*'[21]

Below: French cuirassier officer. (Print by Martinet.)

ORGANISATION

Whereas infantry was generally organised in regiments, each of which might comprise a number of battalions, independent tactical units which might not serve with the remainder of the regiment, each cavalry regiment was generally complete in itself. It is not intended to describe any particular national organisation in detail, but certain factors were almost universal. A cavalry regiment, though usually serving on campaign as a single tactical entity, was divided into sub-units. These were necessary for administrative reasons, but each was capable of independent action on the battlefield: each regiment comprised a number of squadrons, and each squadron was usually composed of two troops or companies. These could also be subdivided, as in the Prussian system in which each troop comprised two platoons (*Zügen*). A squadron or a troop might be detached for some specific duty on campaign, and a common practice was to leave one squadron at

Right: The evolution of
hussar uniform, as worn
in the French Army; left to
right: 1680; 1760; 1794
(Hussards de la Morte);
1810 (1st Regt.); 1824;
1840. (Print after Charles
Vernier.)

Below: Lancers: a trooper
of the 2nd (ex-Dutch) or
'Red' Lancers (Lanciers
Rouges)(left), and a
Lithuanian Tartar (right),
both of the French
Imperial Guard.
(Engraving by Lacoste &
Moraine.)

home to act as a depot for supply of replacement personnel and mounts, but otherwise a cavalry regiment usually took the field entire. If organisation was fairly standard, strengths were less so; a regiment might vary from, for example, the Austrian *Chevauxleger* regiments of 1809 with eight squadrons and a reserve squadron, with an establishment of 1,479 men and 1,414 horses, to a 'field' strength, on campaign, of very much less: the average British regimental strength at Waterloo was 437, for example, and only 354 at Salamanca.

TRAINING AND HORSEMANSHIP

The importance of training in the production of a proficient cavalryman was paramount, and took considerably longer than that required to produce an adequate infantryman. As Wellington observed: 'The formation and discipline of a body of cavalry are very difficult and tedious, and require great experience and patience in the persons who attempt it ... at the same time that nothing can be more useful in the day of battle than a body of disciplined cavalry, nothing can be more expensive, and nothing more useless, than a body of regular cavalry, half and insufficiently disciplined.'[22]

The vital ingredient of horsemanship was often difficult to instil, especially into recruits who had no previous experience of horses (one reason why those who were horsemen already, such as some of the Hungarian hussars or Cossacks, were such a vital asset, sometimes ready for almost immediate service as soon as assembled). Marmont stated that a cavalryman and his horse should be so at one as to resemble a centaur, and as Austrian regulations stated, a cavalry which could not ride was merely a burden to the nation. As was remarked at the time, riding in this sense involved much more than the ability to stay in the saddle and direct the horse in the required direction: but to do that while loaded with equipment, simultaneously using either a firearm or a sword, and often under the most

The Cut against Infantry: a version of the illustration which demonstrated the movement in the British 1796 Rules and Regulations for the Sword Exercise of Cavalry: *the only occasion when a bent arm was recommended, to increase the force of the blow against an enemy at a level below the striker.*

difficult of conditions. Indeed, some held that constant instruction was necessary for cavalry, for if a cavalryman were not advancing in proficiency, he must be retrogressing.

Training applied equally to horses as to the riders, and there are a number of accounts of cavalry horses quite unfit for service: 'not well broke to fire. When *feux de joie* were fired ... a great number of horses were so scared by the report of the pistols, as to run out of the ranks, in spite of all the efforts of their riders',[23] as was reported of a British ceremonial event of 1798. Even worse were occasions when cavalry was needed so urgently that both semi-trained mounts and troopers were pressed into active service, as described by de Gonneville concerning his newly formed French cuirassier unit at Hamburg in 1813. Both riders and horses were untrained, the men very unsteady on first trying to wear cuirasses, and when first ordered to draw their swords, the noise and glitter of the blades so scared the horses 'that they started off like a flight of pigeons, jumping about in all directions and getting rid of their riders, most of whom threw themselves on the ground, when they might have held on longer'.[24] It took two hours to collect the horses, and it was fortunate that their officers subsequently had time to undertake some proper training, or disaster would have occurred in the face of the enemy; as their commander admitted, at first he thought that he could only escape disgrace by getting himself killed!

As in so many cases, anecdotes can be found to contradict the accepted realities; despite the imperative of horsemanship, in Egypt in 1801 a boatswain from the 80-gun ship of the line *Tigre* made a considerable impression upon witnesses by charging enemy infantry while mounted on an ass, from which he fell repeatedly, but still managed to wreak considerable havoc while swinging a cutlass from his improvised 'charger'! The fact that personal skill was not sufficient to produce effective cavalry is exemplified in the succeeding sections on the cavalry's service, for the ability to act in concert was equally significant. This was demonstrated most graphically in accounts of the Russian campaigns against the Ottoman Empire, when it was observed that when Russian officers challenged Turks to single combat the latter were usually victorious, by having the skill to position their horse on the left flank of their adversary, which a cavalryman could only defend with difficulty. When four or five Russians kept together against a similar band of Turks, however, it was the Russians who were usually the victors.

Cavalry combat: British dragoons and French cuirassiers engaged at Waterloo, showing both cut and thrust in operation, and with protagonists literally grappling hand-to-hand, as was described at the time. (Engraving by R. Havell after I. M. Wright).

CAVALRY EQUIPMENT

SWORDS

The great Russian commander Alexander Suvarov remarked that his preference was to fall upon the enemy as soon as he appeared, with whatever forces God had sent: the cavalry to hack, slash, stab and drive, and not give them a moment's respite. While this might be an extremely simplistic view, it represents the opinion advanced by Marmont, that the cavalry's principal purpose was to attack the enemy and engage hand to hand. To that end, the most important part of a cavalryman's equipment was his sword.

Cavalry sabres existed in a great variety of patterns, but the basic design depended upon the two theories concerning the most effective mode of employment of the cavalry sword: the cut or slash, and the thrust. This principle applied to virtually all armies, despite the fact that one Austrian writer recalled the old adage that Spaniards thrust, Germans hack, French guard, but Turks cut to pieces!

Consequently, the preferred method of employment dictated the design of the sabre. To execute a cut, it was held that more weight was needed on the blade, to assist the downward slash, whereas a heavier hilt assisted a thrust by helping to raise the point. Although a cut could be made with either a straight, heavy blade – such weapons sometimes known by the German term *Pallasch* – or with a curved blade, the thrust was delivered most effectively by a straight blade with sharpened point, though it was also possible to deliver a thrust with a curved, pointed blade. Maurice de Saxe, whose writings were held in high regard long after his death in 1750, believed that the sabre 'should be three square [i.e. triangular-sectioned like a bayonet] and carefully blunted on the edges, that the soldier may be effectually prevented cutting with it in action, which method of using the sword never does execution'. Others concurred: 'There can be no doubt that thrusting is the proper use to make of the sword; it is a brutal operation; that is not our business ... we only wish to see our cavalry efficient.'[25]

Karl Emanuel von Warnery, the Prussian cavalry general whose *Remarks on Cavalry* was published in an English translation in 1798, nine years after

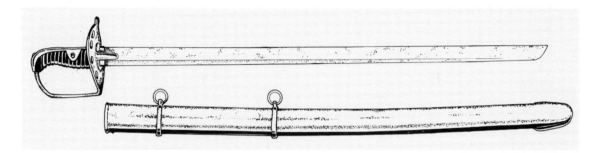

his death, and who based his opinions on his experiences in the Seven Years War, stated that the thrust was preferable because by using the point it could be delivered at a greater distance from the enemy, and with more certainty of causing a disabling wound. It was also remarked at the time that although it was as easy to 'guard' with a straight sabre as a curved one, raising the arm to deliver a cut could expose the body to a thrust, with potentially fatal consequences.

The preference for the thrust was far from universal. Marmont advocated the straight sabre for heavy cavalry, because the thrust was more effective against infantry; but thought that a slightly curved sabre was more useful for single combat, so preferred it as the arm of light cavalry. These distinctions, in fact, were almost universal, with heavy cavalry carrying straight blades and the light, curved.

This theory was reinforced, in rather more detail, by the British *Rules and Regulations for the Sword Exercise of Cavalry* of 1796:

> The *thrust* has only one mode of execution ... a greater degree of caution is required in its application against cavalry ... for if the *point* is parried, the adversary's blade gets within your guard, which is not to be recovered in time ... for which reason the point should seldom or never be given in the attack, but principally confined to the pursuit, when it can be applied with affect and without risk. The case

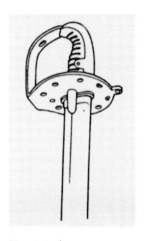

Top: British Heavy Cavalry sabre, 1796-pattern. This heavy weapon with pierced disc hilt was copied directly from the Austrian 1769–1775-pattern which the designer, John Gaspard Le Marchant, had seen in use in the Netherlands. This original version had a hatchet-pointed blade, latterly often converted into a spear-point; the langets were also often removed. All fittings were iron.

Above: Hilt of British 1796 heavy cavalry sabre

Left: French An XI-pattern light cavalry sabre, sometimes known as the 'Chasseur' sabre. Brass hilt, iron scabbard.

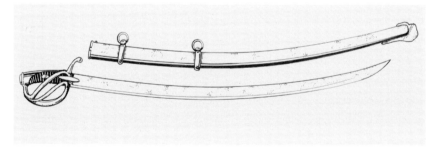

Right: French An IV-pattern hussar sabre, a design derived from weapons as early as the 1752-pattern; brass fittings, scabbard brass and black leather with iron 'drag' or shoe. The original design inspired the weapons of other armies, for example the British 1788 light cavalry sabre and the US sabres manufactured by Starr in 1798 and Rose in 1808–9.

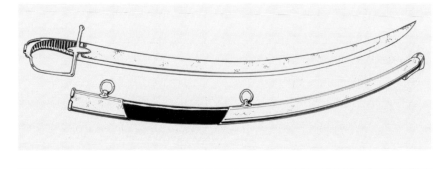

Right: French heavy cavalry sabre, An XIII pattern. This, and the similar An XI pattern for heavy regiments, represent a classic pattern of thrusting sword, with a relatively narrow, pointed blade and brass barred hilt. Subsequently the blade became even more pointed and had more pronounced double fullers. For cuirassiers it had an iron scabbard, for dragoons leather with brass chape, throat and suspension-ring locket.

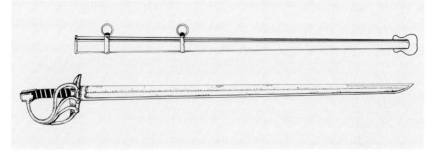

Above right: French An IV Chasseur sabre with its distinctive brass barred hilt, with leather scabbard with brass fittings. Although generally replaced by the subsequent An XI sabre, it continued in use at least with the 2nd Chasseurs à Cheval and for a short time was even carried by elements of the Grenadiers à Cheval of the Imperial Guard.

is different in acting against infantry, as the persons against whom you direct the *point* are so much below your level, that the weight of your sword is not so felt; consequently it is managed with greater facility than with an extended arm carried above the level of the shoulder … against infantry, the point may be used with as much effect as the edge and with the same degree of security.

The complexity of the above exemplifies the fact that to become a proficient cavalryman, a trooper had to be taught almost to fence while on horseback, to deliver blows of different types while protecting his head, breast, back, bridle-arm, sword-arm and thighs, against enemies at right or left, at his level or below him. This resulted in the specification of a whole range of cuts – for example emphasised by the 1796 treatise quoted above – while it was stated that all movement should come from the shoulder and wrist, and be executed with a stiff elbow (so as not to expose the forearm to the enemy's

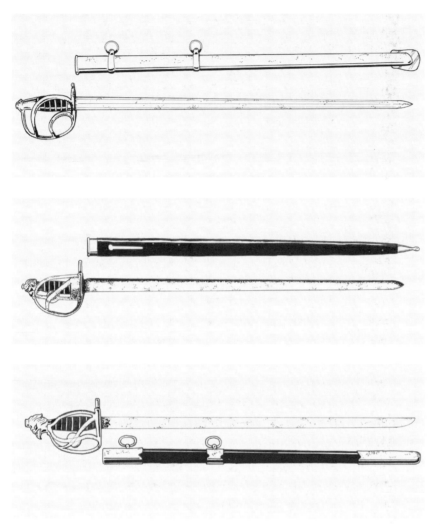

Left and below: The different theories of employment were exemplified by the change in Russian heavy cavalry sabres. The original Dragoon Pallasch had an unfullered blade and semi-basket hilt with lion-head pommel, and leather scabbard; the cuirassier sword was similar but with eagle-head pommel and brass scabbard with leather inserts. (Dragoons of the Caucasian Inspection carried curved sabres). In 1806 the dragoons adopted instead French-style sabres with fluted, 'thrusting' blades with brass triple-bar guards and leather scabbards, and the cuirassiers adopted the same in 1809, with iron scabbards.

Left: Prussian Dragoon sabre, 1797. Representative of an older style of brass semi-basket-hilted swords, the 1797 sabre was based upon the pattern of 1735, but with the alteration of double- to single-edged blade and with the addition of iron lockets to the leather scabbard.

cut), though a bent elbow was necessary against infantry to obtain a sufficient sweep for an effective blow.

The issue of different swords for different types of cavalry was exemplified by those carried by the French. Although they made use of some heavy, straight-bladed weapons akin to the German *Pallasch* (for example the *An IV* carabinier sabre), the predominant types were either straight sabres with relatively narrow blades and multi-barred semi-basket hilts used by the heavy cavalry, or light cavalry sabres with curved blades but sharpened points capable of executing a thrust, initially with stirrup- or single-bar guards, and later with multi-barred hilts. (The designation of weapons according to the year of the Revolutionary calendar used from 1792 to 1805, ranging from *An I* to *An XIV*, indicated the year of the design

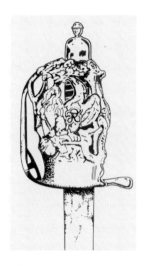

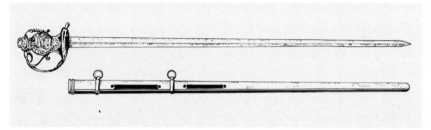

Above: *Prussian cuirassier officer's Pallasch. The straight-bladed sabre with brass semi-basket hilt was a style used from 1732, the double-edged blade changing to single-edged in 1797. The hilt bore a Prussian eagle, grasping a sceptre, below a crown; the same motif was carried on the less elaborate hilts carried by other ranks.*

Above right: *British Household Cavalry officer's sabre, with brass hilt and scabbard. This demonstrates the common practice of copying foreign styles: it was apparently based upon the Prussian Pallasch but had a deeply-fullered blade like that of French heavy cavalry. A number of varieties of this weapon are recorded, including earlier examples with hilts resembling the Prussian style rather more closely.*

of a particular pattern, not necessarily the year of issue, because it was a common practice for old equipment to be used up before new patterns were issued. Thus the *An XI* light cavalry sabre – ostensibly 1802–3 – was probably not issued until about 1807, for example).

Similar variations were found in most of the principal armies, the heavy cavalry using straight blades and the light, curved. The design of hand-guard varied from a simple 'stirrup' consisting of a single 'knucklebow', to basket hilts which largely enclosed the hand in a brass cage; the latter for the *Pallasch* might include solid plaques which might be emblazoned with coats of arms or similar devices. While protecting the hand from sword-cuts, the weight of such hilts might affect adversely the balance of the weapon. An intermediate design, used for example on some Austrian weapons, was a single knucklebow incorporating a folding bar which could be swung out to provide extra protection. At the other end of the spectrum were the so-called 'Mameluke' hilts of the curved, eastern-style swords which became popular with the officers of some armies following the Egyptian campaign; they possessed no knucklebow at all, but merely quillons set at right-angles to the hilt, providing a minimum of protection.

Sturdy leather gauntlets also provided some degree of protection; for example, when the British officer Thomas Brotherton was wounded in single combat with a French officer, he received a cut on the forefinger of the bridle-hand which prevented him from playing his violin for some weeks; yet its force was sufficiently absorbed by the gauntlet to prevent at least one finger from being severed. The contest was decided when Brotherton delivered a thrust – not an effective blow with the curved light dragoon sabre – which he believed had but slightly wounded his opponent. He was much upset to learn of the man's death from the injury, for while engaged in the fight the Frenchman had kept up a cheerful and very polite conversation![26]

Other elements of the sword-fittings had a practical use: scabbard and sword-knot. Metal scabbards were the most sturdy, but had a serious defect in that movement of the blade within the scabbard could blunt the edge,

33

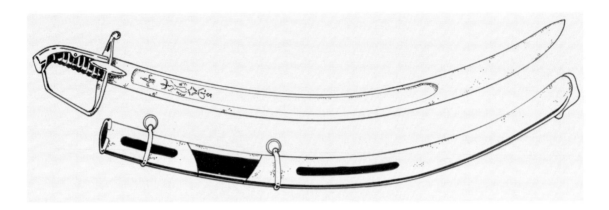

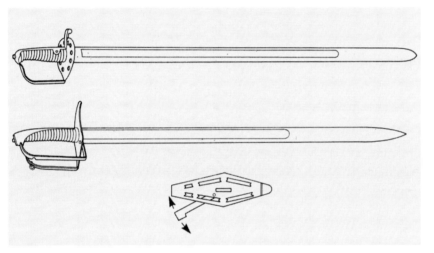

Above: Austrian hussar sabre, 1768 pattern. A classic example of light cavalry sabre, this was carried by the descendants of the original hussars, the Hungarian light horse whose expertise was a great asset to the Imperial (Austro-Hungarian) army. Iron hilt, wooden scabbard with iron fittings and leather inserts; the fittings were brass for senior NCOs.

Left: Top: Austrian 1803-pattern heavy cavalry Pallasch; based on the 1769–75 pattern sabre, including the iron, pierced disc hilt, the 1803 model had a pointed blade instead of the earlier hatchet tip. Bottom: Austrian sabre with folding guard, with detail of how the extra bar could be swung out from the knucklebow to provide enhanced protection for the hand.

and in wet weather might even cause the sword to become rusted in. Leather scabbards, often with wooden lining and invariably with metal reinforcements (throat, chape and suspension-ring lockets were the most common) kept the edge sharper, but were less sturdy. It is likely that oriental swordsmen were able to deliver such fearsome blows, easily capable of amputating a limb, not just because of their mode of executing a cut with a curved-bladed sabre, but because their scabbards permitted a razor-sharp edge to be maintained, whereas such edges were not common in European warfare. The sword-knot, a loop of leather or cord tied to the hilt and usually ornamented with a tassel or leather tag cut in that shape, was not just a method of rank-distinction (officers having lace knots) but fulfilled a very practical purpose. When the sabre was drawn the sword-knot was affixed around the wrist, so that the weapon would not be lost if knocked from the hand, and it also permitted firearms to be used while still keeping the sabre drawn, at maximum readiness, suspended from the wrist.

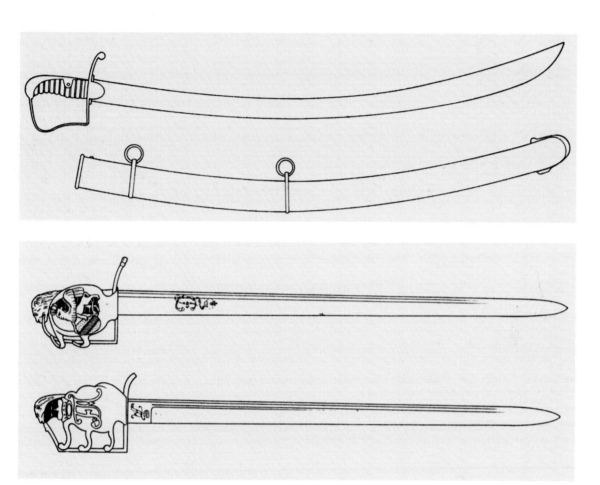

Top: British 1796-pattern light cavalry sabre; with broad blade, designed primarily for the cut, it had iron fittings and scabbard. The design was copied for the Prussian 1811-pattern sabre.

Above: Examples of typical Pallasch-style sabres, c.1800: top: Baden dragoon officer's sword, the brass hilt incorporating the state arms; bottom: Saxon cuirassier officer's sword, the brass hilt bearing the cypher of Elector Friedrich August (King Friedrich August I from 1806).

The need for cavalry to be equipped with the most effective sabre was exemplified by the changes introduced in the British cavalry. They began the French Revolutionary Wars with the 1788-pattern light cavalry sabre, supposedly neither sufficiently heavy nor curved to execute a decent cut, and a variety of heavy cavalry sabres with straight blades and semi-basket hilts, but ill-balanced, and both manufactured of inferior steel. The deficiencies became obvious when compared to the weapons (and the skill in using them) of the Austrians alongside whom the British served in the Netherlands in 1793–4, who John Gaspard Le Marchant observed were 'as superior to us as we are to the train-bands in the city'.[27] It was noted that some of the sabres were so heavy that they twisted in the hand, so that cuts landed with the flat of the blade and delivered only a bruise, and that not only were many horses injured about the neck and ears by their own riders' swords, but the riders wounded themselves by accident, like a friend of Le Marchant's who severely cut his own foot in a mêlée. 'Full of the importance

35

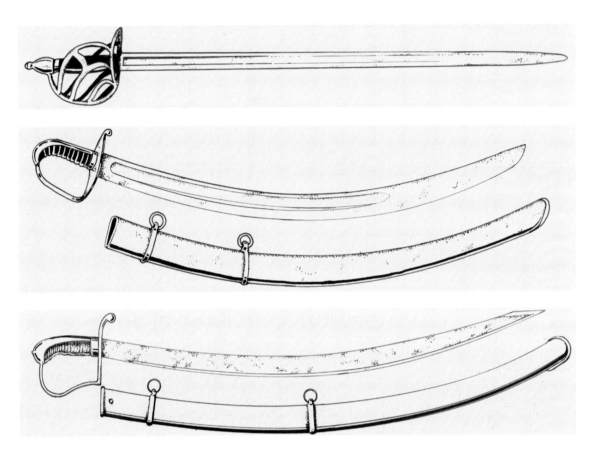

of providing a remedy for so serious an evil',[28] Le Marchant took lessons from an Austrian sergeant and set about improving both weapons and training. The result was both the 1796 manual, and new sabres. The heavy cavalry pattern was copied directly from the Austrian 1775-pattern heavy cavalry sabre, and featured a wide, straight blade and a pierced 'disc' hilt. Originally it had a

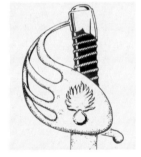

Left: French An IX version of the other ranks' sabre for carabiniers, including the distinctive brass guard bearing a grenade device. The earlier An IV had a similar hilt but with only two bars; for officers the hilt was similar but with more elaborate piercing to the guard, though a number of varieties existed. Blades straight, or very slightly curved.

blunt or 'hatchet' point, so that it could only properly execute a cut, but in 1815 the regiments engaged in the campaign in Flanders were ordered to grind their blades to a point, it was said so that they could take on the armoured French cuirassiers. The 1796 light cavalry sabre had a heavy, curved blade with a wide point not designed for the thrust, so that like the heavy version its intended use was for a cut; and like that of the heavy sabre, its stirrup-hilt guard was made as light as feasible to improve balance. It must have been regarded quite highly as it was copied by Prussia for their 1811-pattern light cavalry sabre.

Top left: British 1788-pattern heavy cavalry sabre, an ill-balanced and unpopular weapon which led to the designing of the 1796-pattern sabre. A number of variations existed in the design of the iron semi-basket hilt; leather scabbard with iron fittings.

Centre left: Austrian hussar sabre, 1803 pattern. Of somewhat simplified construction when compared to earlier patterns, it retained the classic configuration of stirrup hilt and broad, curved blade; iron hilt and scabbard.

Lower left: US cavalry sabre, Model 1813. Two contracts in 1812–13 produced sabres of slightly different specification, but both based upon the British 1796 light cavalry pattern, albeit without langets and with a distinctively shaped point to the blade. Iron fittings and scabbard, which was japanned black.

Right: Cavalry equipment: left: French light cavalry sword-belt, sabretache and sabre of An XI pattern; centre: hussar officer's sabre of typical design; right: typical 'Mameluke' sabre.

There was, nevertheless, still some criticism of the British patterns when compared with the swords of their opponents.

The French dragoon has a long straight sword, the handle is heavy and the blade light, which by adjustment the point is naturally raised without effort, while it feels light and manageable in the hand. The chasseur sabre, though not quite so long, and slightly curved, is, in point of fact, much the same as the heavy dragoon sword, as it is equally applicable to the thrust and is equally handy. The sword of the British heavy dragoon is a lumbering, clumsy, ill-contrived machine. It is too heavy, too short, too broad, too much like the sort of weapon with which we have seen Grimaldi cut off the heads of a line of urchins on the stage. The old light dragoon sabre ... is constructed in utter defiance of Marshal Saxe and his reveries, and as nearly as possible the reverse of what he suggests. We can answer for its utility in making billets for the fire.[29]

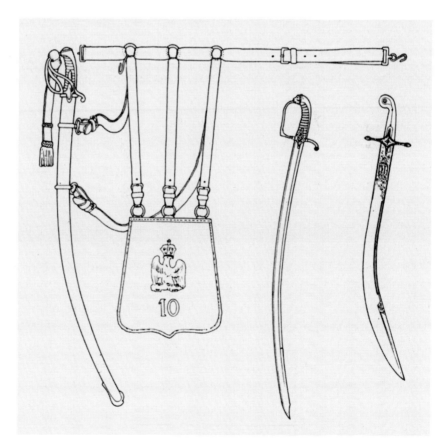

In the debate on the relative merits of different swords, some notice was taken of the combat at Usagre, in which the three French regiments engaged (4th, 20th and 26th Dragoons) carried the straight-bladed dragoon sabre, and their British and Portuguese opponents – and perhaps the Spanish also involved – were armed with sabres principally designed for the cut. While the French were soundly beaten, it was remarked that the greater proportion of their casualties were wounded, while the British suffered a greater loss of killed to wounded, which was taken as evidence that the thrust was more immediately lethal than the cut. (Precise statistics, however, are difficult to ascertain and to evaluate, despite the contemporary comments: French losses were probably about forty killed and as many as 200 wounded, but some of these, at least in the view of the British commander, William Lumley, were caused by artillery fire, while the British loss was perhaps too small to provide a reliable statistical base: Lumley described his victory as 'almost bloodless'.[30]

Even though the thrust may have been potentially the more deadly blow, the cut could produce appalling injuries. It was not merely an unscientific chop; the British 1796 manual, for example, specified six precise cuts and eight 'guards', though the precision with which they might be delivered in the stress of combat is questionable. (The author of the manual, Le Marchant, believed that only the six inches at the end of the blade need be sharpened, to deliver an effective cut without becoming too closely entangled with the opponent). A number of accounts tell how a man might literally be decapitated by a backhand slash, and George Farmer described the dreadful nature of such combat:

A French officer ... delivered a thrust at poor Harry Wilson's body; and delivered it effectually. I firmly believe that Wilson died on the instant; yet, though he felt the sword in its progress, he, with characteristic self-command, kept his eye still on the enemy in his front; and, raising himself in his stirrups, let fall upon the Frenchman's head such a blow, that brass and skull parted before it, and the man's head was cloven asunder to the chin. It was the most tremendous blow I ever beheld struck; and both he who gave, and his opponent who received it, dropped dead together. The brass helmet was afterwards examined by order of a French officer, who, as well as myself, was astonished at the exploit; and the cut was found to be as clean as if the sword had gone through a turnip, not so much as a dint being left on either side of it.

Right: French swords of the Revolutionary Wars, including republican symbols incorporated in the guards. (Print after 'Job'.)

Below: French dragoon officer's sabre, featuring what is sometimes styled a 'bataille' hilt. Originating during the Ancien Régime, the pattern continued in use during the Napoleonic period; it was also carried by chasseurs. Gilded hilt with distinctive, pierced shell-guard, leather scabbard with gilt fittings, and usually a very slightly curved blade, sometimes styled 'à la Montmorency'.

Right: Austrian heavy cavalry sabres. Top to bottom: 1769-pattern; 1769-pattern for NCOs (with brass or gilded hilt and leather scabbard); 1803-pattern; sabre with folding guard.

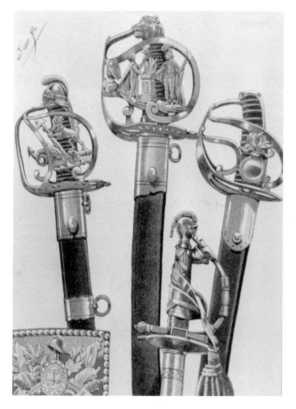

Above: Officers' swords often diverged from the regulation pattern: this example of the British 1796 light cavalry sabre includes a lion-head pommel, chequered bone grip and gilded fittings.

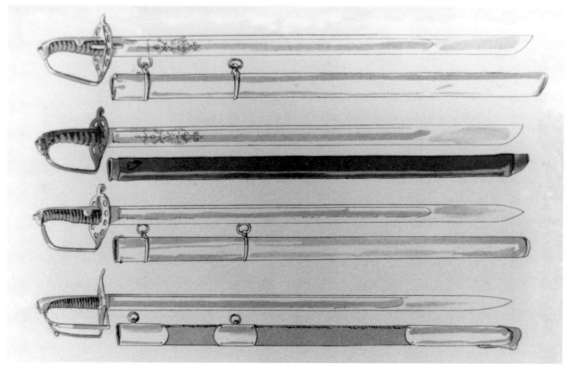

Above: Sword-drill, showing a cut and guard, performed by the Warwickshire Yeomanry, 1801. (Print by C. Williams after E. Rudge.)

Farmer also believed that the cut was more damaging to enemy morale than the thrust; referring to French casualties caused by British sabres, he observed that 'the appearance presented by these mangled wretches was hideous ... as far as appearances can be said to operate in rendering men timid, or the reverse, the wounded among the French were thus far more revolting than the wounded among ourselves'.[31]

Perhaps the last word on the debate between advocates of the cut or the thrust was made by Frederick the Great, who remarked to Warnery that he could kill his enemies either way, it didn't matter which!

Training in swordsmanship included, for the thrust, attempting to hit a ring suspended from a post as the trooper rode past; and for the cut, against targets consisting of a turnip atop a post. (It was against one of these that Sir Walter Scott was seen, saying to himself 'Cut them down. The villains, cut them down!' as he made his blow against his imaginary Frenchman!) Important though the design of swords was, it was the ability to use the weapon which was crucial. An extreme example of how a skilled swordsman could fight with almost anything was quoted in relation to Major William Sewell, an officer on Beresford's Portuguese staff, near Orthes in February 1814. Suffering from a liver complaint, Sewell found it difficult to wear a sword and was unarmed when, 'on learning that the enemy were in our

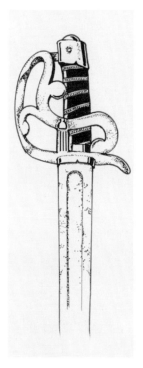

Above: French Dragoon sabre, An IV pattern. The distinctive iron (also brass) scroll-shaped guard incorporated a republican symbol, a sylised Phrygian cap or 'bonnet of liberty' atop lictors' fasces. Straight blade, leather scabbard with iron chape and lockets.

Top right: 'The Austrian Sword-Exercise', performed standing in the stirrups and with a sabre in each hand, as performed by a Mr Goldham of the Loyal London Cavalry. (Print by S.W. Reynolds after W. Wolstenholme.)

front, and that we were likely to have something to do, not being able to borrow a weapon, he drew a stick out of the fence by the road-side'. With this he took on and defeated two chasseurs in single combat, 'and only relinquished the combat when a third had cut his club in twain!'[32]

LANCES

During the Napoleonic Wars the lance enjoyed a considerable renaissance, though opinions on its effectiveness remained divided. Once very common, its use had declined almost to nothing by the middle of the seventeenth century in western Europe, though it continued to be used towards the east, and it remained a favourite weapon in Poland, whence its use spread. A very few lance-armed units were maintained by the western European powers in the eighteenth century, such as the *Bosniaken* of the Prussian Army, which had been raised for Saxony by an Albanian jeweller named Stephen Serkis, who recruited men from the Ukraine. Unable to enlist in Saxon service, he offered his men instead to Frederick the Great, who attached a squadron to his 5th Hussars in 1745, and the unit expanded until it was numbered as the 9th Hussars in 1771. It was the fashion to clothe such units in uniforms resembling their traditional costume, and such was the case when Polish-style lancer units began to be formed by a number of western European armies. In French service, lancers were included in the Polish Legion formed in Italy in 1799, which was transformed into the *Légion Polacco-Italien* for Westphalian service in 1807. In the following year it became the Vistula Legion in French service, including two lancer regiments, and in late 1809 Napoleon had lances issued to his regiment of Polish *Chevau-Légers* of the Imperial Guard, which had been created in March 1807. A second regiment of lancers was added to the Imperial Guard in 1810 (from the old Royal Guard of the Kingdom of Holland, which nevertheless was given Polish costume of *czapka* and *kurtka*: headdress of traditional Polish style, and jacket with plastron). In 1811 nine regiments of line lancers were formed by the conversion of dragoon regiments and the 30th *Chasseurs à Cheval* and the incorporation of the two Vistula Legion regiments. The new units were styled *Chevau-Légers-Lanciers* and were intended to provide a light cavalry element to perform the reconnaissance and skirmishing tasks of the heavy cavalry divisions, a function they fulfilled in the 1812 campaign.

Similarly, lancer regiments were created in some of the other principal European armies. Austria, for example, formed its lancer regiment after the acquisition of the Polish provinces, followed by three others in 1798, 1801 and 1813. Russia converted existing Polish and Lithuanian regiments of Light Horse to lancers in 1803, the number of regiments rising to twelve. Prussia expanded its *Uhlan* (lancer) arm to three regiments and a squadron in the Guard, and five more regiments were converted in 1815. The Prussian case exemplifies how regiments might be armed with the lance but not bear the titles *Uhlan* or *Lancier*: the Prussian *Landwehr* cavalry, raised during the 'War of Liberation', carried lances, and similarly it became a fashion in other armies to equip units of light cavalry with lances though retaining their original designation. In some cases, only a part of a regiment would be equipped with lances, usually carried by the front rank only, as in the case of the Russian hussars, for example, or by a single company (such as that added to the French 31st *Chasseurs à Cheval* in November 1813).

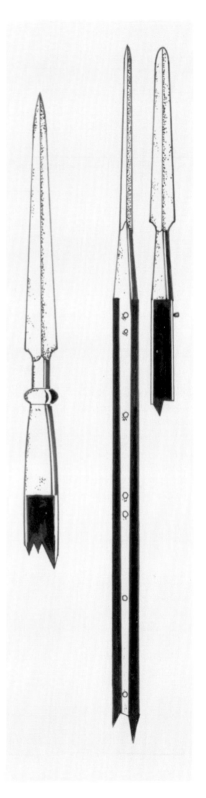

Left: *French lance: the 1807 pattern had a flattened 'ball' beneath the point, which was omitted from the 1812 pattern.*

Many commentators were convinced that the lance was an effective weapon only when used for specific tasks and by small units, if at all. Generally it took a considerable time to train a proficient lancer, one reason, perhaps, why it had fallen out of use: as Cruso's *Militarie Instructions for the Cavallrie* had remarked in 1632, the weapon was 'a thing of much labour and industry to learn'![33] This was one reason why men trained to use the lance from boyhood, notably the Cossacks, were such a valuable resource. The problem was exemplified when the French 3rd Hussars were issued with lances experimentally in 1800–1, evidently without proper training, when it was reported that they were not armed but merely carrying poles! Conversely, when the front rank of Russian hussar regiments received their lances before the 1812 campaign, it was remarked that they soon became proficient enough to use the weapon against enemy skirmishers, and it was also noted that they became more confident by virtue of carrying a lance, which gave them a perceived advantage.

This advantage was not marked when engaged against cavalry, for it was held that except in unusual circumstances, once a lance-point was 'turned' or a blow delivered and missed, the lancer was terribly vulnerable to a swordsman. There was, however, a marked difference between single combat and a general mêlée, and the weapon's merits were argued by exponents of both lance and sword. In trials between a single lancer and a swordsman, both expert, on well-broken mounts and on level ground with ample space, it was demonstrated that the lancer had the superiority, even without the bonus, applicable only in actual combat, of being able to spear his opponent's horse. Apart from the lance-point, the shaft could be used with good effect:

> There is hardly any horse that could be brought again to face the lancer, or even prevented from turning short round, and completely exposing his own rider to the attack, when once it had received upon the nose one of those tremendous blows which can be given with the staff of the lance by swinging it round with the whole strength of the arm, and by means of which men who are good masters of the weapon will actually strike a man clean off his horse if they get a fair stroke at him in this manner.[34]

This was certainly proven by the dexterity with which Cossacks could almost 'fence' with the lance and use their horsemanship to put the enemy at even further disadvantage.

*2nd (Dutch or 'Red')
Lancers (Chevau-Légers-
Lanciers) of the French
Imperial Guard, c. 1812.
(Print after Lalauze.)*

In a more general combat, however, the advantage was reversed, and it
was remarked that an indifferent lancer was 'a much more clumsy fellow'[35]
than an indifferent swordsman: his weapon was more difficult to manage
and his ability to control his mount suffered accordingly, and if the horse
were not perfectly trained, the terrain uneven and the mêlée confused and
thronged with combatants, the inequality was even more marked. A further
drawback of the lance in combat was the possibility that once embedded in
the foe it could prove difficult to extract, and might even deprive the lancer
of his weapon until he could dismount and disentangle it. The French
General Antoine de Brack, who wrote the manual *Avant-Postes de Cavalerie*

Légère (1834: English translation *Light Cavalry Outposts*, London, 1876), based on his service in the Napoleonic Wars, described how a lancer might have to drop his lance, recalling how one of his men let go his lance when it went through a Prussian, who staggered away with it still in him. When the opportunity arose, the lancer dismounted and had some difficulty pushing it out of the now dead body. The first pattern of lance issued to Napoleon's Guard lancers had a flattened 'ball' below the blade which might have helped overcome this problem, but this feature was omitted from the 1812-pattern lance.

The pennon, either when flying or rolled around the shaft, might have served to inhibit such over-penetration, but when used in combat must have exhibited a fairly awful aspect (the regimental tradition of the British 16th Lancers in having 'crimped' edges to their pennons is said to commemorate the Battle of Aliwal, when the pennons became crumpled and stiff with blood). A further advantage of the pennon was that its fluttering could terrify the enemy's horses. This fact was remarked upon, for example, by Thomas Dyneley in the Peninsula: how when fighting lancers, the pennons 'frighten the horses, and they go about and the lancers have them [the riders] through the body in the "twinkling of an eye"'.[36] (Dyneley was evidently writing from hearsay because he described the lancers as wearing brass helmets, obviously confusing them with dragoons). The lance and pennon may also have been used for signalling, and at Quatre Bras another use was recorded. So high were the crops that the enemy was hidden from the view of the cavalry ordered to charge them, and thus the timing of the charge was difficult to calculate. Some bold lancers rode forward, almost on to the bayonets of the infantry, and planted their lances in the ground, presumably butt-first and with pennons fluttering above the corn, to mark the exact position of the troops they were to attack.

Some of the harshest criticism came from British commentators. With the exception of an ephemeral corps of *émigré* cavalry (the *Hulans Britanniques* which existed 1793–6), no British unit used lances until the fashion spread after the Napoleonic Wars, the first British lancer corps being converted from light dragoons in 1816. Perhaps as a consequence, a number of British witnesses were dismissive of the weapon. For example, writing of a skirmish in the Peninsula in 1811, William Tomkinson noted: 'The Lancers looked well and formidable before they were broken and closed to by our men, and then their lances were an encumbrance ... we had only one person ... hurt with a lance, and when retiring, they got on the ground, caught in the appointments of other men, and pulled more dragoons off their horses than anything else.'[37] William Swabey concurred: he remarked that the pennons made 'a very pretty tournament appearance, which effect is quite lost when they are single. They owe their reputation to having destroyed a great many of our infantry when their ranks were broken at Albuera, but as to their being formidable to formed troops it is quite ridiculous; a dragoon with his broadsword is worth two of them.'[38] Even the most expert lancers were at a disadvantage in a mêlée: Baron de Marbot recalled how at Polotsk his 23rd Chasseurs engaged the Russian Guard Cossacks and lost a good many men as they tried to penetrate the phalanx of 14-foot lances, held very straight; but once among them, they had such an advantage of the unwieldy lances that the Cossacks were forced back and lost heavily.

That such opinions were widespread seems confirmed by the fact that Napoleon came to restrict the use of the lance, even in the Imperial Guard, the most famous of the French lancer regiments: from April 1813 the front rank only carried lance, sabre and pistol, the second rank sabre, pistol, carbine and bayonet; *brigadiers* (corporals) in both ranks also carried the carbine and bayonet. It was also suggested that Napoleon was intending to deploy individual lancer squadrons instead of in regiments, to be attached to infantry divisions, to act as orderlies and in reconnaissance, and in action to wait until the enemy infantry was broken and vulnerable to lancer attack. Marmont was another who advocated a radical change in the use of the lance, intended to maximise its effectiveness against infantry. He claimed that the lance had been used by Cossacks and 'Arabs' out of necessity, they having no other weapons, and because they were light cavalry, then it was light cavalry which received lances in other armies. He thought that as the lance was most effective against infantry, it should be carried by the front rank of heavy cavalry, to break up infantry formations by over-reaching their bayonets, whereupon the second rank, armed with straight sabres, could get among them.

Under certain circumstances, the lance could be used effectively against cavalry. A famous case occurred on the day before the Battle of Waterloo, when the French vanguard pursued the retiring Anglo–Allied army from Quatre Bras and through Genappe. French lancers packed into the narrow main street of this town, their lances presenting an impenetrable barrier; their flanks were secured by buildings, and the wet weather precluded the lancers from being broken-up by musketry. The Allied cavalry commander, the Earl of Uxbridge, launched his own regiment (7th Hussars) in an attack

*Lancer of the Austrian 1st
Ublans, 1815. (Print after
R. von Ottenfeld.)*

*Lancer of the Austrian 1st
Ublans, 1815. (Print after
R. von Ottenfeld.)*

against this vanguard, despite the unfavourable circumstances. The sabres of
the hussars were unable to make any impression upon the phalanx of lances,
and they were driven off with heavy loss; one of the 7th's officers, William
Verner, remarked that they might as well have tried to charge a house.
Undeterred, Uxbridge ordered the 1st Life Guards to make a renewed
attempt, which *was* successful, and the lancers were thrown back. It was

suggested that it was the Life Guards' heavier horses which had made the difference – and that the 7th Hussars could have done the same had not their mounts been exhausted from skirmishing – but the decisive factor was probably that the lancers had begun to debouch from the cover of the houses, and thus were open to attack in the flank. One commentator used the incident to criticise the lance, remarking that 'once in actual contact with a lancer, it matters little on what like of horse you are mounted; because, the long unwieldy two-handed lance, at all times ridiculous on horseback, is totally useless the moment you close with the gewgaw champion who bears it'.[39] (The lance, of course, was normally used one-handed.) Even some lancers recognised the limitations of their weapons; de Brack recalled that on two occasions when faced by other lancers, he broke their formation with carbine-fire and charged with the sabre rather than use his own lances.

Against infantry, however, the lance was extremely effective. Infantry were very vulnerable unless formed in square, and if attacked by cavalry when in line or skirmish-order might try to escape by throwing themselves prone, escaping the slash of a sabre from mounted men unable to reach sufficiently low to deliver an effective blow, and relying upon the natural reluctance of horses to tread upon them. Against lancers, however, there was no escape, as men could easily be speared upon the ground; and it was perhaps from this practice, in part at least, that some lancers had a bad reputation, as if stabbing a man on the ground were a dishonourable act (which, if the soldier were capable of standing up and resuming the fight subsequently, it was surely not). Some lancers, however, seem to have regarded wounded enemy soldiers as equal targets; for example, several witnesses of the retreat of the Union Brigade after its first charge at Waterloo, pursued by lancers, recalled how the latter rode at dismounted and wounded men, spearing them unmercifully. Alexander Dickson recalled how dismounted men tried to ward off lance-thrusts with their hands, and some of the wounded must have been speared quite deliberately time and again: some casualties survived a dozen lance-wounds and Sergeant-Major Matthew Marshall of the 6th Dragoons recovered from nineteen distinct injuries. Incidents which tended to sour the reputation of lance-armed troops included the killing, at Quatre Bras, of Sir Robert Macara, stabbed in the head as he was being borne away, wounded, and of Major Edward Hodge, at Genappe, lanced to death while a prisoner there, when it appeared that he might be rescued by a British charge. Similar incidents led one veteran to condemn the weapon as too brutal for 'civilised' warfare:

I trust no British soldier will ever use the lance as the French used them at Waterloo, for the purpose of putting the wounded to death ... war is dreadful enough as it is, but how much more terrible would it be, if no quarter was given to those who should fall into the power of their opponents; and yet to this state of things the employment of Lancers evidently tends. I trust the various governments may be induced to take the matter up, with the view of abolishing the use of the lance in battle.[40]

The classic example of the devastating potential of an attack by lancers occurred with the destruction of Colborne's Brigade at Albuera. Sent forward somewhat injudiciously in line, in a storm of rain and hail and with visibility further obscured by gun-smoke, the brigade seems not to have seen two French regiments – 2nd Hussars and 1st Lancers of the Vistula Legion – until they were actually overrun. It is difficult to ascertain exactly what proportion of casualties were inflicted by the cavalry, but in a very few minutes the 1/3rd Foot had lost eighty-five per cent of its strength, the 2/48th almost seventy-six per cent, and the 2/66th was also ridden down. This action produced more stories damaging to the reputation of lancers, of

Lancer of the Young Guard element of the 2nd Chevau-Légers-Lanciers of the French Imperial Guard (the Young Guard squadrons wore blue jackets instead of the more familiar regimental scarlet). (Print after 'Caran d'Ache': Emmanuel Poiré.)

Lithuanian Tartar of the French Imperial Guard, 1812, wearing the somewhat cossack-style uniform of that corps; he is using his pistol to skirmish while carrying his lance.

the stabbing of men lying prone (whom the cavalry may not have been able to recognise as wounded, if any were); but there was less excuse for the behaviour of one lancer, who seeing a wounded British officer, William Brooke, being escorted to the rear by two French infantrymen, deliberately cut him down and tried to make his horse trample him. (Brooke's life was saved when he was rescued by other French soldiers, who escorted him to safety: he remarked that he thought all the lancers were drunk!)

Such events demonstrate the lethal potential of lancers against broken infantry, even if the statistics are somewhat distorted by the fact that the losses include men taken prisoner. Against infantry in square, however, under normal circumstances lancers had not much advantage over ordinary cavalry, for as one commentator remarked, even a lance three times as long would not reach the infantry before their musketry took effect, and even if the lancer did manage to spear a man in the front rank, he would be shot by the rear ranks before he could do more damage. (De Brack recalled how, in exasperation at not being able to break the British at Waterloo, one of his men threw his lance like a javelin into one of the men in the square.)

Under certain conditions, however, the lancer had a huge advantage over men in square: in weather so wet that muskets could not be fired. Marbot recalled how, at the Katzbach, his 23rd and the 24th *Chasseurs à Cheval* were confronted by a Prussian square unable to fire because of the rain, and the cavalry unable to get up speed because of the sodden ground. The chasseurs walked up to the square and cut at the musket-barrels without effect, until: 'The position on both sides was truly ridiculous; we looked each other in the eyes, unable to do any damage, our swords being too short to reach the enemy, and their muskets refusing to go off.' The situation was resolved when the French 6th *Chevau-Légers-Lanciers* arrived; with their lances they overreached the hedge of bayonets and stabbed an opening in the square (their colonel, Perquit, calling in his thick Alsatian accent, '*Bointez, lanciers, bointez*'), into which the chasseurs rushed and won the day.[41] A similar incident occurred shortly after, at Dresden, when Austrian infantry defied French cuirassiers with bayonets alone, rain having made their firearms inoperative. The cuirassiers were powerless until General Latour Maubourg ordered up his escort of fifty lancers, who stabbed an opening in the square into which the cuirassiers rushed.

Among the most skilled exponents of the lance were the Cossacks, many trained in its use from boyhood, and also especially effective in that they often declined to engage formed troops, but preferred the hit-and-run tactics of the guerrilla, and the riding-down of scattered infantry, circumstances in which the lance was most effective. Other species of pole-arm were carried by 'irregular' cavalry; the Mamelukes, for example, included short javelins in their formidable personal armoury. Another weapon used by Spanish guerrillas was commented upon, a light, short pike similar to those used by picadors in bullfighting (from Spanish *pica*, a lance). Many of Don Julian Sanchez's force who used such weapons, it was said, had been bullfighters and thus were extremely skilled in its use, a case being quoted in which a guerrilla lancer ran his weapon clean through an enemy soldier and also speared the man standing in the rank behind.

It is perhaps worth remarking that some lancers seem to have possessed a higher *esprit de corps* by virtue of carrying the weapon, which they regarded with the greatest pride. A graphic example was quoted by the British gunner officer Cavalié Mercer, who on the day after Waterloo came upon a severely wounded French lancer named Clement, who was sitting among his fellow-wounded exhorting them to bear their suffering like men: 'his suffering, after a night of exposure so mangled, must have been great; yet he betrayed it not. His bearing was that of a Roman ... I could not but feel the highest veneration for this brave man, and told him so, at the same time offering him the only consolation in my power – a drink of cold water and assurances that the wagons would soon be sent round to collect the wounded. He thanked me with a grace peculiar to Frenchmen.' Mercer then turned his attention to the man's lance, stuck in the ground beside him, and begged it as a keepsake: 'The old man's eyes kindled as I spoke, and he emphatically assured me that it would delight him to see it in the hands of a brave soldier, instead of being torn from him, as he feared, by those vile peasants.'[42] Such was Clement's pride in his lance, which he had carried through several campaigns, that he was pleased to see it in the hands of an enemy, and not dishonoured by the hands of scavengers. Mercer had his groom carry it through the rest of the campaign, and in 1827 it was used as a reference by the committee proposing to redesign the British Army's lance. Mercer recovered it after this process and ever after, on Waterloo Day, he stuck it in his lawn, garlanded with roses, as a tribute to the brave man who had carried it in battle.

ARMOUR

In some ways the last link with the armoured knight of the middle ages, the cuirassier of the Napoleonic era was the only soldier of his generation to wear protective body-armour. During the eighteenth century the progressive 'lightening' of cavalry, and the expense and difficulty of finding sufficient horses to mount armoured regiments, had led to a great decline in the use of the last vestige of protective armour, the cuirass. Men so accoutred, being insufficiently mobile to skirmish effectively, were of most use as a striking-force on the battlefield, using their weight and impetus; so that cuirassiers best fitted into those armies large enough to permit some regiments to be reserved exclusively for that role. (Although this was not the only way cuirassiers could operate, *en masse*: the French 13th Cuirassiers, for example, served with distinction in the Peninsula even though they were the only cuirassiers deployed by Napoleon in that theatre.) Of all the principal European armies, only Austria maintained a force of cuirassiers throughout, though even there the number of regiments had been reduced from twelve to eight by 1802. In Napoleon's army, where the cuirassier formed one of the most enduring images of the period, cuirassier regiments were only formed in 1802–3, only one of the previous heavy cavalry regiments – styled *Cavalerie* – having worn the cuirass (the 8th, styled *Cavalerie-Cuirassiers*, the ex-*Cuirassiers du Roi*). In addition to the

French carabinier officer's cuirass. Officers' cuirasses could be very decorative, as in this case: the steel faced with copper, bearing a silver sunburst motif with a copper star in the centre, and silvered shoulder-straps with lion-mask decoration, mounted upon embroidered leather backing.

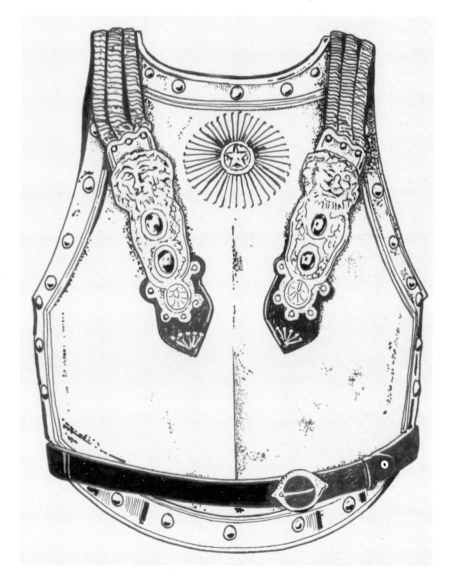

original twelve regiments, three more were formed subsequently: the 13th from provisional troops in Spain, the 14th by the conversion of the 2nd Cuirassiers of the Kingdom of Holland in 1810, and the 15th in 1813, from the depots of the other regiments at Hamburg.

Protective armour more extensive than the cuirass and helmet was hardly ever worn during the Napoleonic period, and then only in the form of mail-coats and coifs worn by some of Russia's Asiatic auxiliaries, and by the Mamelukes. The artistic tradition by which individuals were depicted wearing full armour was still used in the late eighteenth century, but it was a purely symbolic way of emphasising the regality or nobility of the subject.(Nevertheless, it was reported that when General Manuel Freire entered Barcelona in triumph in 1814, one of his entourage was dressed in full armour.)

It is perhaps surprising that the buff-leather coat, worn in the seventeenth century, had disappeared from use, for its protective qualities were acknowledged. (It was said that one of the last to be seen in European warfare was worn by George Preston, who commanded the Scots Greys in the Seven Years War, on one occasion receiving more than a dozen sword-cuts, not one of which penetrated his buff-coat.) A similar case was recorded in December 1813 at Hasparren, when Thomas Brotherton of the British 14th Light Dragoons had his life saved by a 'buffalo leather cuirass' which he had had made at Madrid, to prevent a repetition of being run through the body, as he had been at Salamanca. On this occasion, of eleven thrusts made at him, eight failed to penetrate the leather, and the other three hit unprotected areas, neck, bottom and right thigh, the force of the most severe (the latter) being partially absorbed by some letters in his pocket.[43] Indeed, though unimpressed by the cuirass, Marmont advocated something similar, claiming that relatively little was required to turn a sword-blow, and even to deaden a musket-shot from a distance or pistol-shot at close range. He remarked on the advantages of the mail coats worn by some oriental troops, considered putting light iron chains on the arms and legs, and recommended especially the sturdy buff-leather coat worn by Castilian peasants, as being a light and serviceable form of protection.

In the event, however, only the cuirass was used to protect the body, and existed in two principal varieties. The type worn by the French consisted of an iron breastplate with pronounced vertical ridge – intended to cause blows or missiles to glance off – and a lighter back-plate, the front-plate extending to just below the waist and both with a padded lining to make it

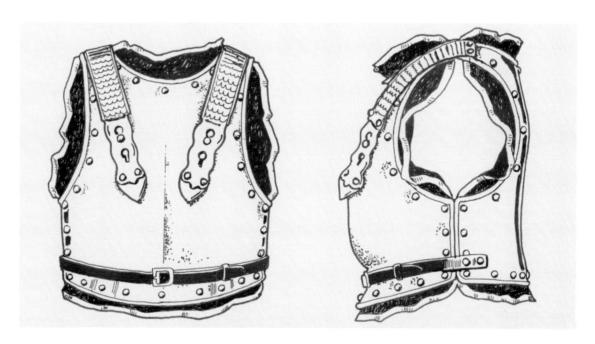

Above: French cuirass for cuirassier regiments: 3rd pattern, 1809. The iron front and back-plates had brass rivets and shoulder-scales.

Right: Austrian cuirasses, consisting of a front-plate only, worn on leather straps which crossed over the wearer's back. The gilded edging and 'dart' at the neck (left) was a rank-distinction worn by officers. (Print after R. von Ottenfeld.)

more comfortable. The plates were connected by a waist-strap fastening around the front and attached to the back-plate, and scaled or chain straps linked the plates at the shoulders. Succeeding patterns were similar, the second type having a more rounded front lower edge and the third, introduced from 1809, a more pronounced ridge. Brass-faced cuirasses were issued to the two Carabinier regiments when they were 'armoured' in 1810.

The second type of cuirass consisted of only a front-plate, worn on leather straps. Although Austrian cavalry had worn complete cuirasses – and seventeenth-century-style, lobster-tailed iron helmets – in 1788–9 when campaigning against the Turks, for European warfare they wore only the front-plate, enamelled black. In Russia,

An artistic convention intended to emphasise the nobility of the subject, especially prevalent in the eighteenth century, implied that cuirasses were worn more frequently than was actually the case. This portrait of King George III by C. H. Küchler is a good example; this particular medal was used as a regimental award by the Duke of Gloucester's Loyal Volunteers in 1805.

although the heavy cavalry were called cuirassiers, they only received body-armour in 1812, generally full cuirasses but also some with just the front plate. These too were usually enamelled black, but variations included the Pskov Regiment which wore captured French cuirasses in white-metal (brass for officers), and the officers at least of the Empress Regiment also wore white-metal. Despite the effective use of the cuirass in Frederick the Great's army, in Prussia it was abolished in 1790 and not re-adopted until 1814–15, despite the continuing use of the title 'cuirassiers'. Most of the later issue were captured French cuirasses, although the Garde du Corps and Brandenburg Regiment were authorised to wear black, and some black cuirasses were presented to Prussia by the Tsar. Some smaller armies also maintained cuirassier regiments – for example the *Regimiento de Coraceros Españoles*, formed in Spain in May 1810 and using captured French equipment – though some may have been created more for reasons of prestige. For example, when Jérôme Bonaparte formed his two Westphalian cuirassier regiments he was criticised by Napoleon, who noted that he had told his brother 'over and over again, that he ought not to have cuirassier regiments, because that branch of service costs too much money, and the native horses are not adapted to it'.[44]

Almost alone of the principal European nations which fought throughout the period, the British never adopted the cuirass, seemingly because troops so accoutred were not able to perform 'outpost' duties, and the British Army generally had too few cavalry to keep any exclusively for 'shock' action on the battlefield. The only British experience with the cuirass was in the Netherlands campaign of 1794, when the Royal Horse Guards received an issue of them (and of iron skull-caps for wear under the hat, like the '*secrète*' of the seventeenth century). These are often stated to have been a re-issue of old stocks, but in mid-1794 one John Davies submitted a bill to the Board of Ordnance for 230 skull-caps and breastplates

French cuirassier. (Engraving by C. A. Powell after Géricault.)

for the regiment, at a cost of £169.1s.0d., for which straps had to be procured at 3s. each.[45] They were found to be too cumbersome for use on campaign and prone to rust, so were returned to store, and a recommendation that all heavy cavalry should wear cuirasses, made by the Board of General Officers convened to comment on cavalry equipment in 1796, was ignored. In 1814, however, a detachment of 2nd Life Guards was equipped with black cuirasses for ceremonial duty, perhaps to enhance their appearance during a visit of the Allied sovereigns to Britain, or as a compliment to the Russian cavalry, but they were withdrawn almost immediately.

Opinions were divided on the use of the cuirass in action. An Austrian writer condemned them as a useless encumbrance, representing extra weight which would only impede the rate of a charge against an enemy already wavering (for against a formed enemy, he implied, no charge should be ordered); and that back-plates were only useful to protect cowards. (The latter point had been made in 1768 by the Marquis de Silva, who remarked that to deprive infantry of a breastplate was contrary to the dictates of humanity, but that a back-plate would only induce the soldier to turn his back on the enemy!)

Cuirasses were certainly proof against musket-shots at longer range (but then a 'spent ball' at the end of its flight would not even penetrate clothing), and the first French cuirasses were supposed to be 'proof' against three musket-shots at thirty paces, but when numbers failed this test the criterion was reduced to one shot at long range.[46] One of the most striking accounts of the protective value of the cuirass involved a Russian officer known as 'Fensch the Second'(to distinguish him from his elder brother; their real name was Fanshawe, of British origin). At Kulm 'Fensch II' – George Fanshawe – tried to help a wounded French officer who was lying in a ditch, and removed the man's cuirass to make him more comfortable. The cuirassier died, however, and seeing that the cuirass was an ornate one, Fensch donned it, presumably as the easiest way of carrying it, intending to show it to the Grand Duke Constantine. After the battle he told the Duke that but for the cuirass he would be dead, as it had turned three musket-balls; Constantine said that it was a clear case of humanity, Fensch's attempt to help the dying Frenchman, having its just reward.

There are, however, many accounts of cuirasses providing scant protection against firearms, one of the most unusual being that of Private Dickson Vallance of the British 79th, who recalled how after Quatre Bras the

British used discarded cuirasses as frying-pans, although 'some of the gravy was lost through the bullet holes'.[47] (He added that some Belgians who saw this reported that the Highlanders were cannibals.) After this battle at least one British commanding officer (Frederick Ponsonby of the 12th Light Dragoons) searched for cuirasses to determine whether they *were* shot-proof; he exhibited one that had been pierced by three balls. Rees Gronow of the British 1st Foot Guards recalled that one of his most vivid memories of Waterloo was the sound of balls striking the cuirasses, which he compared to the noise of a violent hailstorm hitting panes of glass. It was said that the belief that the cuirasses were bullet-proof led to the order given to British troops, when they first met cuirassiers in combat, specifically to shoot the horses, which though an effective tactic was regretted by Gronow at least, who felt more compassion for the horses than for their riders.

The cuirass is shown excellently in this portrait of a French carabinier, c. 1812. (Engraving by M. Haider after Géricault.)

Cuirasses were of greater value in combat against cavalry, both from their ability to turn blows and, in conjunction with the heavier horses, in providing greater solidity and 'shock' as compared to lighter-mounted opponents; a British Life Guard wrote of Waterloo: 'Until we came up with our heavy horses, and our superior weight of metal, nothing was done with the Cuirassiers, unless one now and then got a cut at their faces.'[48] Some suggested that the weight of the cuirass was not conducive to swordsmanship, as Edward Cotton remarked after seeing a wounded German hussar in single combat against a cuirassier: 'The strength of cavalry consists in good horsemanship, and the skilful use of the sword, and not in being clad in heavy defensive armour. The superiority of the hussar was visible the moment the swords crossed: after a few wheels a tremendous facer

The sturdy leather Raupenholm ('crested helmet') used by a number of German states provided a considerable degree of protection; this example is from Württemberg.

made the Frenchman wheel in his saddle, and all his attempts to escape his more active foe became unavailing; a second blow stretched him on the ground.'[49] Cuirasses were also a great handicap when the wearer was dismounted, as Wellington observed at Quatre Bras: 'Those that were not killed were so encumbered by their cuirasses and jackboots that they could not get up, but lay sprawling and kicking like so many turned turtles.'[50] It was for this reason that discarded cuirasses were found on the battlefield; Cavalié Mercer recalled how, after Waterloo, piles of them were used as seats around the campfire, there being 'more cuirasses than [dead] men; for the wounded (who could move), divesting themselves of its encumbrance, had made their escape, leaving their armour on the ground where they had fallen'.[51]

Another argument concerned the merits of the back-plate. Although heavier, a full cuirass may have been more comfortable to wear, if the breastplate were balanced: as early as 1726 General Henry Hawley had remarked that without a back-plate, the breastplate could not be worn with 'ease and pleasure', and that in recent campaigns some soldiers had contrived to lose their front-plate rather than to suffer constant pain.[52] Of equal relevance was the defensive capability of the back-plate. Marbot recalled the great cavalry action at the end of the Battle of Eckmühl, in which cuirassiers of both armies opposed each other in a mêlée so fierce that in the twilight sparks were struck from the iron armour. Here, claimed Marbot, the debate about whole cuirasses as against front-plates was answered, for the French, with no fear of being wounded in the back, could concentrate on offence; and once the Austrians wheeled-about to retreat, 'the fight became a butchery, as our cuirassiers pursued'[53] and struck at their unprotected backs. He claimed that the proportion of Austrian killed and wounded amounted to thirteen and eight respectively for each corresponding French casualty.

Metal helmets also provided a degree of protection, as did the sturdy leather helmets worn by the cavalry of many armies. The high comb, and the high skulls of the German leather *Raupenhelm* (crested helmet) could absorb a sabre-blow from above, if not always a sweeping blow from the side: 'I cut off the half circle of brass formed on the top of the French dragoon's helmet, and it made so great a noise close to the man's head, that he conceived himself to be killed, without being in the least injured. He fell off his horse as if a round shot had struck him.'[54] Those unused to fighting men who wore helmets were sometimes surprised to find cuts to the head having little effect: a story was told of a Sergeant Taylor of the British 18th Hussars at Waterloo, who made a cut at a cuirassier who cried 'Ha! ha!' as it was turned by his helmet. Taylor then thrust his sabre through the cuirassier's mouth and himself said 'Ha! ha!' as the Frenchman fell. Metal helmets were far from invulnerable, however, as demonstrated by George Farmer's story quoted above. De Brack remarked that having seen so many cuirassier helmets cut clean through by sword-blows at Essling, he preferred the protection of a sturdy leather shako. Marmont concurred, recommending that two pieces of wood in the form of a cross be added to the shako (presumably on the crown) to help turn a blow.

The high boots worn by some heavy cavalry were also a form of protective equipment, notably in saving the legs from being crushed in a tightly packed charge – but like the cuirass were a considerable encumbrance when dismounted. Marbot recalled how one cuirassier officer who had been dismounted at Eckmühl found his boots so heavy that he was unable to keep pace with the troops who tried to rescue him. He was found later in the day lanced to death by the enemy while taking off his boots in an attempt to move faster.

Further protection, used by infantry as well as cavalry, was a rolled cloak or greatcoat slung diagonally across the body. It formed part of the regulation mode of carrying the equipment in some armies – notably those of Russia and Prussia – and it was said that among the French cavalry the order 'roll cloaks!' was a sign that action was imminent. Its effectiveness was described by a participant in the Portuguese Civil War of 1832–3: 'This mode of carrying the greatcoat looks well, is convenient to the wearer, and very useful in action, as it protects the most vital parts of the body, viz., the heart and chest; indeed, after an affair with the enemy, it was usual on unrolling the greatcoat, to find that several rifle and musket-balls had lodged in the folds, and thus saved the life of the wearer; in fact, more men were generally killed or wounded when they fought in their greatcoats than when they wore them rolled.'[55]

FIREARMS

Cavalrymen needed firearms when skirmishing, but their effectiveness was often criticised by experienced commentators. Cavalry longarms were usually referred to by the generic term 'carbine', implying a lighter and shorter-barrelled weapon than an infantry musket, but the term includes a wide range of weapons.

The most effective carbines seem to have been those used by the French cavalry, initially the 1786 'musketoon' (of musket-bore) and, after 1801, the *An IX*-pattern carbine. As in many armies, its use was restricted initially to the light regiments which performed most of the skirmishing duties; in general the heavy cavalry did not receive carbines until 1812. This de Gonneville found inconceivable, noting that carbines were quite impossible to use on horseback by men wearing the cuirass, and that they could only be of use if the troops were required to serve on foot. In addition, he dismissed the notion that lancers should carry carbines, and recalled that these had had to be withdrawn when found to be of no use. Similarly, the British cavalry commander Stapleton Cotton ordered carbines to be withdrawn from the Household Cavalry in 1813 (save six per troop, presumably for the use of sentries), on the grounds that such troops were never called upon to skirmish, and that their horses had sufficient weight to carry already. Indeed, some were against the whole idea of arming any cavalry with firearms, one Austrian writer describing it as inconceivable that the cavalry's primary function, that of rushing upon the enemy, should be neglected in favour of ineffective carbine-fire.

French carbines were longer-barrelled than those of some nations, and thus were held to be more accurate, though the short-barrelled types, for example the Austrian hussar carbine (reduced in overall length from 90cm to 85.2cm in 1798 and 76.5cm in 1815) or the British Paget pattern, were a

Austrian hussar trooper, c. 1814. Although in use, the carbine is still attached to the shoulder-belt by means of the spring-clip, so that the weapon would not be lost if it had to be dropped to allow the hussar to use his sabre, itself attached to the wrist by the sword-knot. The ramrod hangs from its strap on the shoulder-belt. (Print after R. von Ottenfeld.)

reaction against the longer-barrelled types which were thought to be too cumbersome for use on horseback. Despite its somewhat limited use, a wide variety of cavalry carbine was available. In British service, for example, the heavy cavalry originally carried the 1770 Heavy Dragoon musket, similar to that of the infantry but with a smaller bore and 42in barrel; the Royal Horse Guards carried the 'Blues carbine' with 37in barrel; and light regiments the Light Dragoon or Elliott pattern (named after General George Augustus Elliott, later Lord Heathfield), with 28in barrel, approved in 1773 and still in use in the mid-1840s when its barrel was reduced to 20in and was reissued to yeomanry. The Heavy Dragoon pattern was condemned as unduly cumbersome in 1796 by the board convened to review equipment, and it was recommended that until a new weapon with 26in barrel be produced, existing carbines should be cut down to that length. A further variation introduced from 1797 was the use of Henry Nock's 'screwless' or enclosed lock, in which the mechanism was concealed behind the lockplate. It had been designed at the instigation of the Duke of Richmond (when

Right: The ability of cavalry to skirmish effectively on foot was significant: French Chasseurs à Cheval, 1809. (Print after Rozat de Mandres.)

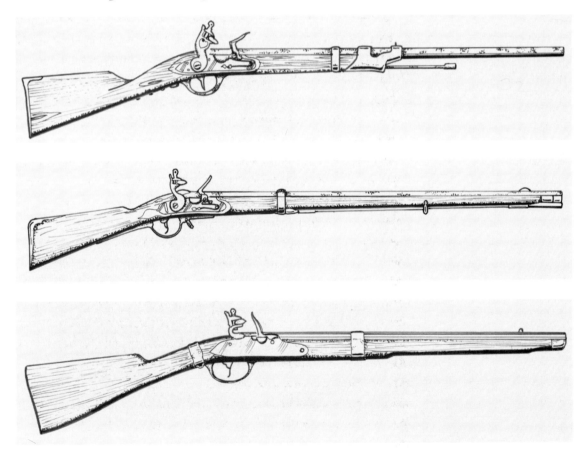

Top left: French 1786-pattern cavalry carbine, designed for light regiments: barrel-length 70.4cm (27.7in), brass fittings.

Centre left: Prussian 1787 heavy cavalry carbine: barrel-length 88.5cm. (34.8in), brass fittings save for iron barrel-band supporting rod-and-ring belt-fitting.

Bottom left: Although perhaps the best-known of its type, Henry Nock's 'enclosed' lock was not unique: a similar design was used on this Danish light cavalry carbine of 1807, and on the cavalry pistol of the same year. The iron bands enclircling the stock supported the usual rod and ring belt-fitting.

Master-General of Ordnance) in 1786 and was intended for an infantry musket, but when this failed to be issued the unused locks were fitted to the carbines carried by some regiments. From about late 1808 the Paget carbine (named after General Henry Paget, later Marquess of Anglesey) was issued to light regiments; it had only a 16in barrel, swivel-ramrod and a 'bolt lock' incorporating a sliding safety-catch.

Another recommendation by the 1796 board was for the introduction of a standard bore for both pistol and carbine, which as the French realised greatly simplified the resupply of ammunition. In British service, for example, weapons of musket-bore – including carbines produced in that calibre – took balls of 14½ to the pound, carbine-bore weapons balls of 20 to the pound, and pistols balls of 34 to the pound. Despite the obvious advantages, however, in the British case the attempt to standardise bores was abandoned. This may have been in an attempt to prevent accidents: even when the bores of carbines and pistols were the same, it was still necessary to use less powder for a pistol, for had a carbine-cartridge been used with all the powder it contained, the recoil from the resulting ignition might have blown the pistol from the hand.

Considerably different was the French dragoon musket, in effect only a slightly shorter version of the *An IX* infantry musket (barrel-length about 103cm instead of the 113.6cm of the infantry version); it was as efficient as the ordinary musket and was carried by some infantry *voltigeurs* as well, its shorter length making it rather more handy for skirmishing.

French cavalry longarms were generally regarded as superior to those which opposed them, probably a combination of the longer barrel and enhanced training and ability, French light cavalry being equally adept at fighting on foot as well as firing when mounted. Combined, these gave what one veteran described as 'vast advantages',[56] used subsequently to advocate the formation of corps of mounted riflemen: 'The French mounted *Chasseurs* gave us enough of trouble.'[57] The comments of Jonathan Leach were probably quite typical: 'The French dragoons and *chasseurs à cheval* were armed with a long fusée, which could throw a ball as far as the musket of an infantry soldier, and our dragoons, on the contrary, were armed with a little pop-gun ... the French dragoons often dismounted ... and shot at our dragoons at a distance which rendered our short carbines almost useless.'[58]

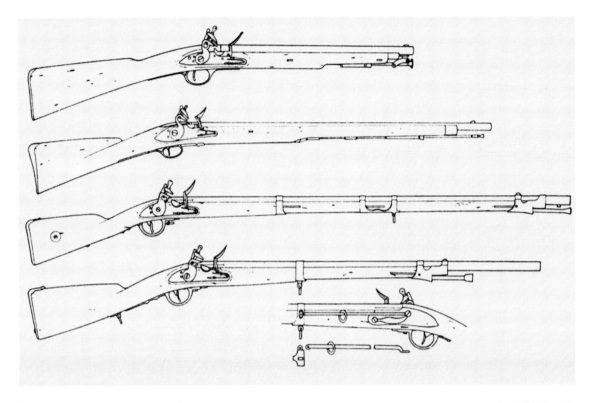

Another commentator thought the French dragoon musket rather too long, but that the 'chasseur carbine' – presumably the *An IX* pattern – was light and capable of throwing a ball at least twice as far as was necessary (cavalry skirmishing was presumably intended to take place at close range). As for the British carbine – presumably the Paget – he stated that 'our light dragoon carbine is so decidedly bad in all respects, that we have only patience to say, the sooner it is got rid of the better'.59 Another weapon which drew similar plaudits to the French carbine was the light musket carried by the Cossacks, which was stated to possess the range of an infantry musket yet weigh much less.

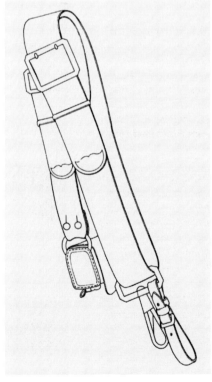

In addition to possible difficulties of ammunition-supply in the field, which might bedevil weapons with a different bore from the norm, some had a problem with the ramrod. Some carbines (of the longer variety) were carried muzzle-uppermost with the butt in a 'boot' attached to the horse-harness, but it was more common for the carbine to be provided with a metal bar and sliding ring on the opposite

Top left: Cavalry firearms: From top to bottom: British 'Paget' carbine (barrel-length 16in (40.7cm), brass fittings) British 'Elliott' carbine (barrel-length 28in (71.2cm), brass fittings); French Dragoon musket, An IX-XIII pattern (barrel-length 102.8cm (40.5in), brass fittings but iron middle band); French cavalry carbine, An IX-XIII pattern (barrel-length 75.8cm (29.8in), brass fittings but iron middle band). The reverse side (bottom) shows the metal rod and running ring fitting on the stock which enabled the weapon to be suspended from a shoulder-belt, a common feature on the carbines of many nations.

Left: French cavalry shoulder-belts, the upper carbine-belt with the spring-clip and leather securing-strap from which the carbine could be suspended, an item of equipment used by many armies.

Right: Austrian hussar carbine, 1798: length 85.2cm (33.6in); brass fittings, but iron barrel-band. The lock has a hooked safety-catch known as a 'dog-lock'.

Bottom right: Austrian Kavallerie-Stutzen (cavalry rifle), 1789: length 69cm (27.2in); brass fittings, and hooked safety-catch on the lock.

side of the stock to that of the lock, so that the gun could be suspended, muzzle-downwards, from a spring-clip on a belt slung over the shoulder. Although the weapon thus remained to hand and safe from loss – it could even be fired without unfastening it from the shoulder-belt – it was easy for a loose ramrod to fall out, as with the British heavy dragoon carbine, when 'nothing was more common than for the soldiers to drop and lose their ramrods altogether'.[60] One solution was to have the ramrods permanently attached to the carbine by means of a swivel mounted near the muzzle, like that of the Paget carbine, but the weight tended to unbalance the weapon. Perhaps a better alternative was to attach the ramrod by means of a leather thong to one of the belts worn by the trooper, so that it was upon his person rather than on his carbine, a system used by the Austrian cavalry.

Another complaint made about the carbine (and applicable even more to the pistol) was that its light weight, when compared to the infantry musket, was insufficient to resist the recoil of a full charge of powder, reduced charges leading to diminished velocity and thus effectiveness. It was observed that in some cases, carbine-balls fitted so loosely that after an hour's riding (obviously with the carbine hanging muzzle-downwards) a troop with 'loaded' carbines might find that many of the balls had simply fallen out, especially if the barrels were clean (barrels fouled with burned powder provided a less smooth route of escape for the balls).

Rifled carbines did not enjoy very extensive use. France, for example, had only the shorter-barrelled cavalry version of the Versailles *carabine* of

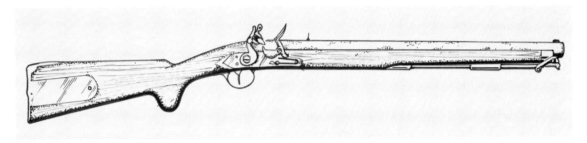

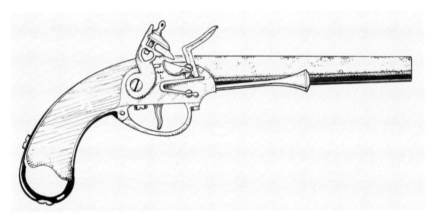

Above: *Baker cavalry rifle. An example of a rifled carbine, this design of Baker, with the pronounced pistol-style butt, was like that carried by the British 10th Hussars. Barrel-length 20in (50.8cm), brass fittings.*

Left: *French 1777-pattern cavalry pistol; barrel-length 18.9cm (7.4in), calibre 17.1mm. Brass fittings; the version shown here has an iron belt-hook which was later usually removed.*

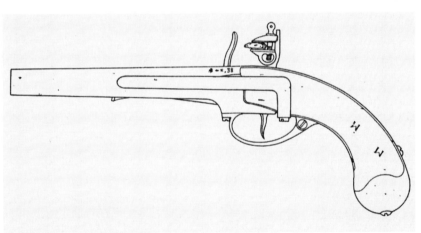

1793 (40.6cm barrel instead of 65cm), which apparently did not enjoy much success, and a rifled musketoon (with 75cm barrel) was produced for the Dragoons of the Imperial Guard. Rifled weapons were usually issued only to selected personnel; for example, in the Austrian cavalry, in 1792 six men in carbine-armed squadrons were issued with the Model 1789 *Kavallerie-Stutzen*, a weapon with a barrel-length of 69cm (in musket-bore; the 1798 version was produced in carbine-bore). Similarly, in the Russian heavy cavalry, only sixteen men per squadron received rifled carbines and were

Right: French An XIII-pattern cavalry pistol; barrel-length 20.7cm (8.2in) calibre 17.1mm. Brass fittings, but with iron reinforcing-straps along the top and underside of the butt.

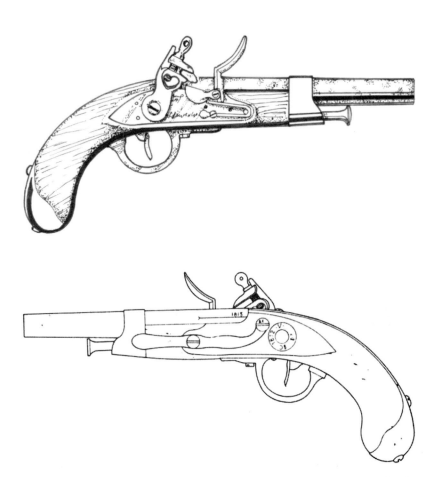

designated as 'flankers'. Only a small number of Baker rifled carbines were issued to British hussars, but it was reported that despite its short barrel-length it proved little inferior, if at all, to the infantry musket (presumably in terms of range). It was certainly effective at times, for example when a detachment of 10th Hussars covered the river-crossing at Thy on the retreat from Quatre Bras, their rifle-fire discouraging any further French pursuit.

Other types of cavalry 'longarm' were used in even smaller numbers, notably short blunderbusses. A small number of these were carried by the Mamelukes of Napoleon's Imperial Guard (79cm overall, with a bell-mouthed muzzle: only seventy-three were produced), and in Austrian service the Model 1759 *Trombon* (blunderbuss) had been issued to twelve men per cuirassier squadron, but was withdrawn in 1798.

Despite the proficiency of French cavalry skirmishers, Marmont declared that firearms in general were almost superfluous, and were of most use as a method of signalling. Excluding dragoons, whom he advocated should be returned to their original function of mounted infantry, he recommended no more than twenty carbines per squadron. This practice was followed by some armies, when only a few men in each troop would carry carbines (and were sometimes styled 'flankers'), though this tended to minimise the importance of the ability to skirmish. This was criticised by some: 'A great number of regiments content themselves with merely selecting in each troop a few of the most active men and horses as permanent skirmishers, to rush out from the ranks at full gallop for mere effect and display, and return, after firing off their carbines half a dozen times in the air, at the same unnecessary speed with which they went out.'[61] Indeed, firing from the saddle cannot have been very accurate if for no other reason than the movement of the horse; 'a man who is a tolerably fair shot on his own legs, may find himself as much puzzled upon a shy or hot-tempered horse, as a horse-artilleryman would be perplexed to take a good aim with an 18-pounder in a heavy sea on board of ship'.[62]

The use of cavalry pistols was even more problematic. Most troopers carried one or two pistols in holsters at the front of the saddle, and they were produced in huge quantities and in a large variety of patterns. In French service, excluding a few regimental types like the pattern produced for the Mamelukes of the Imperial Guard, cavalry carried the 1777 pistol, characterised by its small amount of woodwork and a steel ramrod at the side of the barrel, until the issue of the *An IX* pattern. This had a stock extending almost to the muzzle, with the subsequent *An XIII* pattern reverting to a foreshortened stock. The British, conversely, had a wider range of patterns, barrel-lengths and bores, including the Heavy Dragoon

Right: British Light Dragoon pistol; brass fittings, barrel-length 9in (23cm).

Below: US Harper's Ferry pistol, Model 1805: barrel-length 10.06in (25.2cm), brass fittings. The first official US pistol was the Model 1799, based upon the French 1777-pattern, and from 1807 fully stocked pistols were authorised, notably the Model 1811 (based on the French An XIII pattern but with barrel secured by pegs) and the Model 1813 (the same but with iron barrel-band).

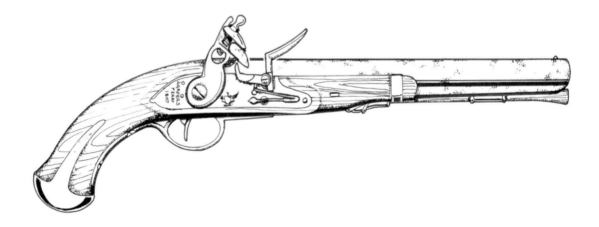

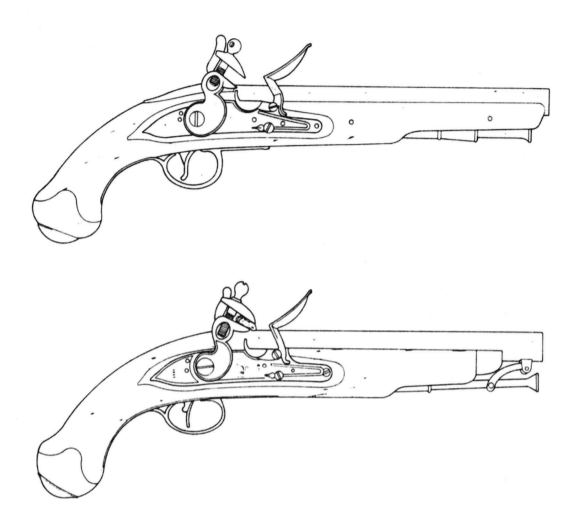

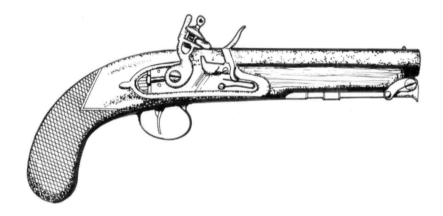

Above: *British New Land Pattern pistol, with ramrod attached by a swivel; barrel-length 9 in (23cm).*

Right: *Privately purchased pistols of superior manufacture were often carried by officers: this London-made example features a chequered butt (to aid grip), a safety-bolt on the lock, and the swivel ramrod so useful for service on horseback.*

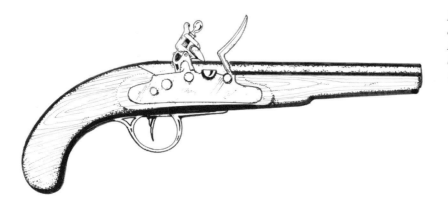

Left: British 1796-pattern cavalry pistol, fitted with Nock's enclosed lock; barrel-length 9in (22.8cm), brass fittings.

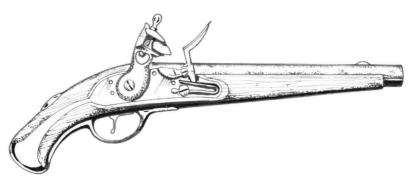

Left: Russian cavalry pistol, of Tula manufacture, 1814; barrel-length 26.8cm (10.5 in), brass fittings.

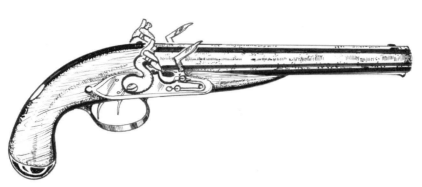

Left: Though not common, double-barrelled pistols were used; Henry Nock supplied some to the British Royal Horse Artillery in 1793, with a 'shifting' (removable) shoulder-stock and one rifled and one smoothbore barrel. This British cavalry example was carried by the Bedford Light Dragoons: side-by-side barrels 10.25in in length (26cm), two locks and triggers, brass fittings.

pistol (12in barrel, pistol- and carbine-bore); Light Dragoon (9in barrel, carbine-bore); Life Guards (10in barrel, carbine-bore); Royal Horse Guards (10in barrel, pistol-bore). The 1796 board recommended a new universal pistol of musket-bore and 9in barrel, of which some were fitted with Nock's lock and others with a swivel-ramrod like the Paget carbine, but it was not popular and by 1801 the previous Light Dragoon pattern was being ordered again. The problem of losing the ramrod when firing from horseback applied as much to the pistol as to the carbine, unless attached by a swivel, or by a leather thong to the trooper's belt; the unpopular British 1796 pistol

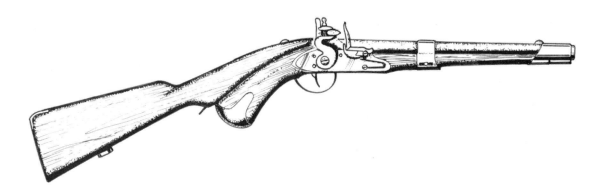

Above: Pistols could be turned into carbines by the addition of a shoulder-stock, as in this Swedish cavalry pistol, authorised in 1807 and produced in both rifled and smoothbore versions. Detachable shoulder-stocks also existed in 'skeleton' form, with the centre cut out to reduce weight; for example, one such was designed by the Earl of Ancram for his Midlothian Fencible Cavalry.

carried its ramrod in the holster. Even worse, in combat the pistol might be dropped in the haste to replace it in the holster, if the trooper needed to use his sabre with urgency, which led one commentator to advocate the practice of the Cossacks, of carrying the pistol on a long cord over the shoulder; after firing, it was simply thrown over the shoulder, out of the way of the sword but safe from loss.

Some commentators at the time followed Marshal Saxe's opinion that the cavalry pistol was only a useless addition of weight, and one recalled the German belief that a pistol should not be fired until 'you feel your antagonist's ribs with the muzzle. Why not then use the sword? ... We never saw a pistol made use of except to shoot a glandered horse', and that 'it would be difficult to produce a cavalry soldier having on any one occasion fired his pistol at an enemy'.[63] Nevertheless, there certainly are recorded instances of pistols being used in combat, and not only by individual officers (who might procure their own weapons, which could be considerably different from the regulation patterns). Some may even have preferred to use a pistol rather than a sabre; for example, Lieutenant William Turner of the British 13th Light Dragoons recalled a charge at Waterloo in which 'I shot one Frenchman with my pistol but did not use my sword (I had the misfortune to break the double-barrelled one in marching up the country or else I should have shot two).'[64] At Dresden there occurred an example of how pistols could be useful in particular situations: when rain prevented infantry from firing and made the ground too heavy to allow cavalry to work up a charge. In this case, French cuirassiers broke an Austrian infantry formation by riding up and shooting with their pistols until sufficient infantry had fallen as to enable the horsemen to get through the hedge of bayonets and engage with the sword. Obviously the cuirassiers' pistols had been kept dry in their saddle-holsters and were thus the only arms that would fire.

Cossacks surprise Napoleon's escort on the day after the Battle of Maloyaroslavets and come near to capturing the Emperor. (Print after J. V .Chelmioski)

CAVALRY SERVICE

SKIRMISHING

The possession of firearms enabled the cavalry to perform skirmishing and similar duties, an important if sometimes neglected part of their service. It was often carried out on horseback, and indeed some seem to have been especially inept at skirmishing dismounted; for example, it was observed: 'A British dragoon when placed upon his mother earth, looks very much like a fish out of water. He seems half ashamed of the pedestals that nature gave him; and to think that the only legitimate way of overcoming an enemy, is either by riding him fairly down, or by cleaving him handsomely in twain from top to bottom.'[65] Those fully adept at all kinds of skirmishing – like the French light cavalry and dragoons – had a distinct advantage over their opponents. Austrian observers were especially impressed by the French *Chasseurs à Cheval* whose carbines enabled them to act as light infantry, evidently with only a few of their number acting as horse-holders, the men linking bridles to prevent their mounts from straying. When their opponents threw out their own skirmishers to oppose them, the chasseurs immediately mounted and cut them up with their sabres, before the opposing troops could react.

The techniques of skirmishing were similar to some degree, and a fairly standard practice was described by the British regulations. Skirmishers, it stated, should be at least 200 yards in advance of the main body and should form two ranks, with officers and NCOs between them to direct their movements. In advancing, the front rank would fire, then the rear-rank men would advance through the gaps between them, ride forward fifty yards further and themselves only fire when what was now the rear rank had reloaded; so that, as with infantry skirmishers, at least one of every pair of men was always ready to fire and thus cover his comrade. In retiring the same process was undertaken in reverse, so that the whole formed a kind of caracole. It was emphasised that loading should take place on the move, and that skirmishers should never cluster together, so as to present as small a target as possible. It was said that it was easier to fire to the left, but that men should also occasionally fire to the right; and the regulations

A Cossack, apparently armed with a British 1796-pattern light cavalry sabre. (Print after Horace Vernet.)

made the fairly obvious points that at the moment of firing the skirmisher should not apply his spurs to his mount (and thus unsteady his aim), and should take the greatest care not to hit or burn the horse's head with the flash of the carbine.

When preceding a charge, it was laid down that skirmishers either rejoin their own squadrons in the charge, or retire and rally together at the rear; though in some armies the skirmishers continued to operate upon the flanks of the charge. Some regulations emphasised the need for skirmishers always to be supported closely by a body of cavalry, ready to charge if the skirmishers should be attacked, to which end it was recommended that never more than a minority of men be employed in skirmishing; the Saxon regulations of 1810, for example, limited the number to not more than one-quarter of the whole. There are also many accounts of individual troopers acting virtually alone, loading and firing in their own time. One such incident was recorded at Waterloo, in which a lone French cavalryman rode forward several times and fired his carbine, each time waving it around his head and shouting abuse in English, until eventually he was himself shot off his horse. Probably due to the difficulty of shooting from horseback, however, much skirmishing, especially at longer ranges, seems to have been relatively bloodless; for example, it was remarked that the cavalry skirmishing which occurred on the extreme right of Wellington's line at Waterloo seemed to be singularly without effect.

Inadequate training was the cause of much ineffectual action by many troops employed on skirmishing, 'outpost', security cordon, patrol and reconnaissance duties, the British being notorious in this regard. For example, in the 1801 revision of *Instructions and Regulations for the Formations and Movements of the Cavalry*, skirmishing occupied only four of 374 pages. One officer observed: 'To attempt giving men or officers any idea in England of outpost duty was considered absurd, and when they came abroad, they had all this to learn. The fact was that there was no one to teach them. Sir Stapleton Cotton tried, at Woodbridge in Suffolk, with the 14th and 16th Light Dragoons, and got the enemy's vedettes and his own looking the same way.'[66] Consequently such duties had to be learned when actually on campaign, though as one commentator remarked, 'to learn to shoot by being shot, is a kind of *instruction mutuel* which can never be made at all palatable!'[67] It was fortunate for the British that their army included the King's German Legion, whose light cavalry was acknowledged to be the 'outpost' experts *par excellence*, exemplified by an officer who, though a cessation of hostilities had been announced at the end of the Peninsular War, still went to bed fully dressed and ready for immediate turn-out. When asked why, considering that an armistice was in place, he replied, 'Air mistress or no air mistress, I sleeps in my breeches!'68 So sketchy was the official British 'outpost' training, in fact, that there was not even a regulated system of signalling, so that in the Peninsula the 16th Light Dragoons had to evolve their own. Upon the appearance of the enemy, a sentry raised his helmet on his carbine and

Modern and ancient arms: a Russian infantryman of 1812 (left), Cossacks (centre) and a Bashkir armed with a bow (right).

A Bashkir displays his bow. (Print after von Kubbeil.)

circled his horse to the left to indicate the approach of cavalry, and to the right for infantry. If the enemy were advancing rapidly, he cantered rapidly in a circle, firing his carbine if not noticed; and if it became too dangerous to hold his post he retired, firing repeatedly.

Cavalry skirmishing was usually carried out with carbines, though there are references to the use of pistols. An example, albeit in somewhat exceptional circumstances, evidently occurred at Hasparren in December 1813, when a party of British 14th Light Dragoons attempted to charge over a bridge only wide enough for two horses to proceed abreast. Being galled by French carbine-fire from across the river, the commanding officer, Thomas Brotherton, in expectation of receiving support, led a charge across the bridge. On the other side the French 13th Chasseurs, who seem to have drawn Brotherton into committing an error, replied by volley-firing with pistols (and presumably continued flanking carbine-fire, though it was pistols which Brotherton mentioned particularly).This brought down the horse of the officer who accompanied Brotherton, who charged into the chasseurs accompanied only by his orderly, and was wounded and captured.

In considering skirmishing, especial note should be taken of the 'irregular' light cavalry *par excellence*, the Cossacks, described with every justification by one commentator as the right arm of the Russian Army. Mounted on small, light and amazingly hardy ponies ('the most surprizing little animals in the universe – the largest of them not more than thirteen hands high – something like our new forest ponies'),[69] the Cossacks formed a priceless asset. 'They and their horses have alike constitutions of iron temper – no toil, no weather, no privation impairs them.'[70] Sir Robert Wilson, who served alongside them, was unstinting in his admiration:

The Cossacks possess an acute intelligence and capacity which belongs only to themselves. By the stars, the wind, and an [*sic*] union of the most ingenious observations, he travels like a bird of migration ... Nothing can elude his activity, escape his penetration, or surprise his vigilance. His main point of honour, beyond even that of courage itself, is never to be surprised, never to offer any advantage to his enemy by his negligence. Mounted on a very little, ill-conditioned, but well-bred horse, which can walk at the rate of five miles an hour with ease, or dispute the race with the swiftest ... armed with the lance, a pistol in his girdle, and a sword, he shuns no competitor in single combat; and, in the late war [1806–7] carried terror and death into every opposing squadron ... The Cuirassiers alone preserved some confidence, and appeared to baffle the arm and skill of the Cossack; but in the battle of Eylau, when the cuirassiers made their desperate charge upon the Russian centre, and passed through an interval, the Cossacks instantly bore down upon them, speared them, unhorsed them, and in a few minutes appeared themselves in the armour of five hundred and thirty of them whom they had strewed on the plain ... it must not, however, be imagined that the Cossacks are suited to act in line, though occasionally successful even in that form. Their peculiar service is in the charge *en masse*, or what in Germany is called the swarm attack, i.e., without any systematic formation, in a crowd, and every man trying to get before his fellow ... The Cossack is not first armed with the lance when he proceeds to war – it is the constant exercise of his youth and boyhood, so that he wields it, although from 14 to 18 feet in length, with the same address and freedom that the best swordsman in Europe would use his weapon.

In reconnaissance and 'outpost' duty, the Cossacks were probably without superiors; a very apt simile used to describe their abilities averred that if light cavalry were the army's eyes, then it was as if the Russian Army was a body studded with eyes which were never closed to sleep. For raiding and harrying an enemy the Cossacks were without equal, their fearsome reputation aiding the panic which often occurred when unsuspecting troops were surprised by their shout of 'Hurrah!' which preceded their hit-and-run tactics. Never was this demonstrated to greater effect than when the Cossacks helped harass the *Grande Armée* out of existence in the Russian campaign of 1812, when the very knowledge of their presence had a profound effect upon their foe. An officer who survived the retreat from Moscow noted that only a few Cossacks were required to disrupt the equanimity of the army. What especially amazed them, he recalled, was the Cossack ability to live on land which the French thought bereft of food or fodder; and the need to escort every minor foraging-party, lest they be ambushed by Cossacks, tired out the retreating army and cost them more

Mameluke cavalry, 1798–9. (Print after Horace Vernet.)

Mameluke horseman skirmishing with his pistol. (Engraving after Horace Vernet.)

casualties than a battle would ever have done. Whenever the officers of the rearguard turned around, he said, they would espy one or two Cossacks peeping from behind a tree or a bank, ready to pounce upon anyone who strayed from the main body, so that only a very few Cossacks were needed to keep the troops in a state of constant apprehension.

As Wilson remarked, the Cossacks were not suited to conventional cavalry combat; indeed, another commentator observed that the fact that some despised them for their unwillingness to engage in regular conflict was merely proof that they misunderstood the very purpose of Cossack tactics, and that to train them to act as line cavalry would have been a waste of their natural skills. Even some in the Russian Army seem not to have recognised fully the value of 'Cossack warfare'; for example, General F. P. Uvarov was criticised for not seriously engaging the enemy with his corps, and with *Hetman* Matvei Platov's Cossacks, which operated on the army's

right flank at Borodino, whereas in fact the very presence of this force, and the fear engendered by the presence of the Cossacks, caused the paralysis of much of Napoleon's left and centre for a crucial part of the day. Although there were many accounts of how formed troops could easily drive off Cossack marauders, there were occasions when the latter pressed their attack in the open field. An incident occurred in 1813 when a numerically inferior band of Cossacks caused considerable disorganisation among a French cuirassier formation by engaging its flanks and rear with carbine-fire and lance-thrusts, the French hardly being able to combat them despite having some of their flank- and rear-files turn outwards.

Set against their unquestioned attributes, the Cossacks had a formidable reputation for plunder: 'of predatory habits, a cruel horde of plunderers, preying alike on friends and foes, when they can rifle the

A Mameluke: a contemporary engraving which emphasises the ornate nature of the equipment of these formidable warriors.

Mamelukes of the Imperial Guard at Austerlitz, the most exotically equipped of all Napoleon's troops. (Print after F. de Myrbach.)

former with any chance of escaping detection ... never restrained in their actions by an inconvenient sense of moral obligations',71 according to one who served alongside them; 'great gluttons, and greater drunkards,[yet] although scarce able to stand, when once mounted, they seldom fail their duty'.[72]

Considerably less formidable were the other irregular cavalry fielded by Russia: Asiatic light horse, often styled Bashkirs and Calmucks; indeed, it was remarked that they were even despised by the rest of the Russian Army (which, it was claimed, would regard eating with one of them with as much relish as if they had to share a meal with a dog!) Nevertheless, they were certainly among the most exotic combatants of the Napoleonic Wars, and provided probably the only instance of the use of archery in Napoleonic warfare. They were armed principally with 'composite' bows and arrows, and, as Marbot described, being as ill-trained as a flock of sheep, their only tactic was to shout and fire their arrows in a parabola as they charged forward, so as not to strike their comrades in front; this deprived the arrows of any real impetus so that they were impelled only by their own weight when they finally came down. The reaction of soldiers when confronted by troops wielding bows and arrows was generally one of contempt, perhaps best exemplified by the actions of a British officer, Lieutenant Henry Stisted of the 2nd Foot when hit in the calf by an arrow at the storm of Ghunzee in July 1838: as his men passed he displayed the leg and recited *Who killed Cock Robin?* to them (*I, said the Sparrow/With my bow and arrow!*) Marbot was similarly dismissive, describing the Bashkirs as the least dangerous troops in the world, whose employment he could never understand, as all they did was consume scarce food. They must have been courageous, however, as he described how they would swarm around their enemy like wasps, undeterred by casualties, and eventually did cause some injuries with their arrows. At Leipzig one of Marbot's NCOs, named Meslin, was shot through from breast to back; he broke the arrow in half and drew the two pieces from his body, but died in moments. It was a rare fatality caused by what Marbot described as 'this ridiculous weapon', though he was himself hit in the thigh by an arrow which penetrated only about an inch. It was because of this weapon that the French nicknamed these irregulars '*les Amours* ' or '*les Cupidons du Nord* ' – 'Cupids'.

Another 'irregular' form of cavalry with a quite unique system of combat were the Mamelukes, as encountered by the French during the Egyptian expedition. Fighting in a manner not far from that of the Middle Ages, the Mamelukes were probably the most heavily armed warriors of the period, though totally without discipline. Their sole tactic was a rapid charge, executed with immense bravery, during which the Mameluke would fire his carbine and the several brace of pistols with which he was equipped, throw his light javelins, and then close with the sabre. Each Mameluke had a number of servants who would follow their master to retrieve the firearms, which were thrown aside after use, and to apply the *coup de grâce* to any survivors of the charge. Often clad in helmets and mail, and including axes, maces and daggers in their personal arsenals, the Mamelukes individually were extremely formidable, but being entirely deficient in discipline and the theory of acting in concert, they could be defeated by formed troops with relative ease.

ON THE BATTLEFIELD

It was often held that the cavalry's prime purpose was to engage the enemy on the battlefield, sword in hand; but within this principle were many variations.

In the early eighteenth century the principal role of regular cavalry was offensive, following its aggressive use by commanders like Gustavus Adolphus, and continued in the armies of Frederick the Great and Maria Theresa. For this purpose cavalry had been concentrated into massed formations, but the development of infantry tactics, and the enlarged size of armies, had tended to shift the balance towards the foot-soldier, so that in

The decorative nature of military uniform and equipment reached its apogee in hussar costume, of which a most magnificent example is depicted in this illustration of an officer of the Guides of the Neapolitan Royal Guard during the reign of Joachim Murat. (Print after L. Vallet.)

some armies cavalry became more of a supporting arm than a primary weapon of offence. During the Napoleonic Wars some armies had such small cavalry contingents that this was inevitable, but the change was also reflected by the tactical deployment of cavalry brigades, often attached to infantry formations rather than in autonomous cavalry forces. (This also reflected the growth in the size of armies: *corps d'armée*, which could act alone and without immediate support, of course needed their own cavalry.) Armies that maintained large numbers of cavalry could still deploy them in large formations, for example the four Reserve Cavalry Corps in the *Grande Armée* of 1812, as well as providing the support element in the divisional and corps cavalry, though even these large formations were more part of an integrated system than providing the main striking-force on their own. An example of the change of emphasis was perhaps represented by the employment of cavalry in Austrian service: by 1813 it was distributed through the army's formations in comparatively small bodies, making the earlier use of large formations difficult to duplicate. This process was compounded by the lack of coverage of multi-regiment charges in the regulations, and of large-scale exercises, and as commanders desired cavalry detachments for flank-protection for their infantry, to some degree it began to take on the aspect more of a support element than the primary striking-force of previous years.

Nevertheless, the cavalry fulfilled a vital role on the battlefield: it could be used to neutralise the enemy's horsemen, pose a threat to an infantry attack, make a breakthrough by exploiting a weakened section of the enemy line, cover a withdrawal or conduct the pursuit of a defeated enemy. To a large degree the ability to perform some of these tasks was dependent upon the organisation and numbers of cavalry available; armies with only small contingents might have to husband their mounted troops, whereas those with large forces could make massed attacks, and use them as 'accelerated infantry', as Wellington described Napoleon's use of his cuirassiers. Perhaps the most outstanding example of the latter occurred at Borodino, when the fortified Raevsky Redoubt was captured by the Saxon *Garde du Corps* and Zastrow Cuirassiers, with Westphalian and Polish cuirassiers, but another example of perhaps more significance occurred at Eylau. There, one of the greatest cavalry attacks in history was made by Napoleon, conducted in appalling conditions of ice and blizzard, but not, as originally intended, to exploit a weakness in the Russian line and deliver the final blow to break the enemy. Instead, so severe was the discomfiture of Napoleon's infantry that he had to use his cavalry to stabilise a critical situation and, in effect, prevent his defeat. This meant attacking troops who were steady and confident, not (as intended) those whose morale was already crumbling from the attention they had received from other 'arms'. That this was achieved, albeit at a considerable price, not only demonstrates the quality of the cavalry involved but also the versatility of large cavalry forces with competent leadership.

Leadership, indeed, was of paramount importance, and required considerable skill, especially when conducting large bodies of troops. Marmont commented upon the difference between commanding infantry and cavalry, in respect of the comparative rates of movement. With infantry, at the speed they marched, a commander had time if necessary to halt or change his plan of manoeuvre, but with cavalry he had to be certain of his course of action from the beginning, because of the rapidity with which his initial orders could be carried out. An error at the beginning of a manoeuvre would be fatal, as it could rarely be rectified, so that cavalry commanders had always to blend boldness and promptitude of decision-making with prudence. It was especially important, stated Marmont, that a cavalry general should husband his resources scrupulously until the time for action came, looking after the needs of both men and horses and, on the battlefield, shielding them from enemy fire until the moment of action, and only then should he commit them, and fully, to gain the maximum effect, irrespective of the casualties they might suffer. This combination of abilities was rare, he thought, and was shared during the Napoleonic Wars by only three of the French commanders, Kellermann, Lasalle and Montbrun. The rest, thought Marmont, were either careful administrators, fearful of sustaining losses in action, or (like Murat) bold in action but so careless of the well-

One of the most Famous cavalry commanders of the period, and certainly the most flamboyant: Joachim Murat (1767–1815), King of Naples, Grand Duke of Berg, and Marshal of France. (Print by Bosselman.)

being of their troops that they were worn out by the preliminary stages of a campaign and thus could not operate to full efficiency on the battlefield. As Napoleon himself remarked, the vital ingredients of cavalry service were audacity and practice, and cavalry should never be dominated by a spirit of conservatism or avarice.

Indeed, the battlefield performance of cavalry was very dependent upon the quality of leadership, which at times was sadly deficient. There were innumerable brave officers of the Murat class, capable of leading a charge or inspiring their men, but even those of distinguished reputation might be deficient in tactical aptitude. The French general Horace-François-Bastien Sébastiani, who took over Montbrun's Corps in the Russian campaign after the latter was killed at Borodino, was an example. His reputation for being caught unprepared led to his nickname 'General Surprise', and Marbot remarked that although he displayed great courage in a fight, he was so careless of reconnaissance even when the enemy was near (spending his time in his slippers, reading Italian poetry) that as a general he was noted only for his mediocrity. Inept leadership could hardly fail to have a bad effect upon morale, as was reported of some British commanders in the Peninsula: as surgeon Charles Boutflower remarked of the cavalry in 1812, 'This lamentable dereliction from what they were is not attributed to any degeneracy in the Men, but to the incapacity, not to add, want of courage, of many of the Generals ... it has become so notorious, that there is scarcely a Dinner party, or assemblage ... where the conduct of our Cavalry Generals is not spoken of with disgust & contempt.'[73] Among the worst was probably Sir John ('Jack') Slade, about whom Henry Paget (later Marquess of Anglesey, one of the best cavalry commanders) once called to an ADC to 'ride after that damned stupid

The most distinguished British cavalry leader of the period: Henry William Paget, Earl of Uxbridge and from 1815 Marquess of Anglesey (1768–1854), commander of Moore's cavalry in the Corunna campaign and of Wellington's in the Waterloo campaign.

fellow'[74] to ensure that he committed no blunder! It was of Slade that William Tomkinson remarked, 'The things said of him by different officers were so gross, that I am certain they would not have been allowed to pass unnoticed had they been applied to any other man in the army.'[75] The need of officers who were tactically astute was not restricted to general officers, but extended to unit-commanders, or else a regiment might be led into confusion. An example was provided in the Peninsula when George Quentin, commander of the British 10th Hussars (whose behaviour caused a wholesale revolt among his officers) went missing when his regiment was under fire and only eighty yards from the enemy. Left without orders, his officers were beset with similar lack of decision: the senior officer present, Major Howard, asked his subordinate, Captain Fitzclarence, 'What shall we do now?'[76]

The speed of march of cavalry was an important factor in determining the progress of a campaign, though this was so dependent upon circumstances that it is difficult to make any firm generalisations. Ralph Adye, whose *Bombardier and Pocket Gunner* was something of a contemporary *vade-mecum*, stated that the 'usual rate of marching' of cavalry was seventeen miles in six hours, 'but this may be extended to 21, or even 28 miles in that time',[77] but over a short period of time this could be exceeded greatly. A considerable feat of marching, for example, was that undertaken by the British 4th Dragoons who rode from Canterbury to London at the time of the Gordon riots, sixty-three miles between sunrise and sunset, and arriving 'in perfect order'. Such efforts could not be sustained, even in the French Army which had a reputation for rapid marching second to none. When Junot marched to Portugal at the beginning of the Peninsular War, for example, he covered 640 miles in forty-three days, the first 300 at twelve miles a day over main roads and the remainder, on minor roads, at eighteen miles a day; but this was so fatiguing that the cavalry and artillery had to be left behind and rehorsed, and arrived at Lisbon ten days later than the infantry.

The cavalry's rate of march was equally significant on the battlefield, though again was governed entirely by circumstances. Adye stated that 'military horses *walk* about 400 yards in $4\frac{1}{2}$ minutes, *Trot* the same distance in 2 minutes 3 seconds, and *gallop* it in about 1 minute'.[78] Such statistics permit calculations to be made regarding, for example, how many rounds of artillery-fire or how many infantry volleys a charge might have to sustain before reaching its target; but in reality factors such as the state of the

Some of the most magnificent equipment was reserved for cavalry musicians: trumpeter of Dragoons, and kettle-drummer of Chevau-Légers-Lanciers of the French Imperial Guard. (Print by Lacoste after Demoraine.)

terrain, the fatigue of the horses and the resolution of the enemy could make such a difference from the theoretical performance that it is difficult to make any kind of generalisation. For the sake of example, if Adye's calculations were valid, if attacking cavalry began to gallop when 250 yards from their target, it would take about thirty-eight seconds to arrive, so that it would be possible, in theory, for infantry to deliver two complete volleys in that time; but steady infantry might well reserve their fire until the cavalry was considerably nearer, so that one complete volley would be more likely, albeit one spread over two or three ranks, or by platoons, so that the effect might have been two or three partial volleys, or a continuous fire from one part of the line or another.

Under normal circumstances, all manoeuvre (on or off the battlefield) was performed in column, and at a pace conducive to the maintenance of order. The British regulations, for example, emphasised that manoeuvres should be conducted at the pace of the slowest horse (noting that very slow horses should not be in the cavalry in the first place). The transition between speeds, it stated, should be made gradually, including 'slow trot', 'quick trot', 'slow gallop' and 'quick gallop', beginning and ending gently, with ordinary manoeuvring conducted at either trot or gallop.

The specific details of how cavalry executed a charge varied between armies, but certain factors were fairly standard. It was often stated that lines were the best formation for a charge (Marmont, for example, that the line was the *only* formation), though, especially latterly, attacks in column became more common; by 1812, for example, both Prussian and Russian regulations recommended attacks by column of platoons or squadrons. The column attack – executed by individual troops or squadrons, or by such formations in succession – was stated to be easier to control with troops who were less well-trained, and became common even in French service in the later years, when out of necessity units had to be sent into the field before their training was complete, and with many young and inexperienced officers. Column attack was also of obvious use against infantry formations of limited frontage, such as the head of an infantry column or a square, against which a cavalry line might overlap to such an extent that the flanks would not be engaged; and they could also be of use against cavalry in the same formation.

The concept of a regimental charge might be misunderstood, and brigade or divisional charges even more so. Although cavalry was most effective acting in larger bodies, most manoeuvres were carried out at squadron level, even in cases involving a regimental or larger charge, so that once it was commenced squadrons might operate independently within the concept of a charge in line, for example. Marmont recommended that cavalry should always act in squadrons, not in larger formations, for the longer the line, the more chance there was of its being disordered by events or in the passing of obstacles; he advocated forty-eight files divided into four sections of twelve each as the best for keeping control. The huge charge of a solid line – sometimes styled *en muraille* (like a wall) – might be intimidating but was so difficult to control that Warnery described it as 'pernicious'!

Operation by squadron also permitted a common variation on the charge in line, that by echelon, in which successive squadrons came into

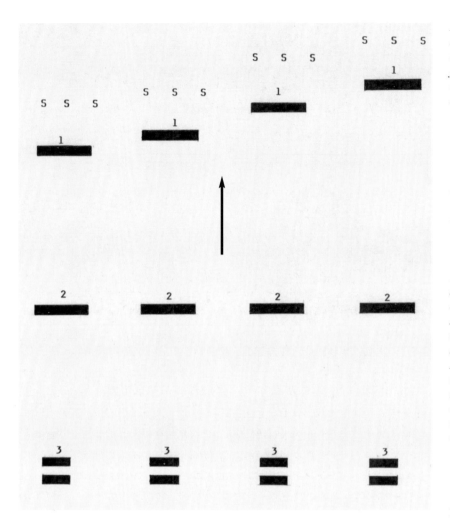

action, one after the other, giving the opportunity for the succeeding squadrons to take advantage of the effect on the enemy of the actions of the preceding squadron, to change their target or to take the enemy in the flank. For example, the *British Military Library or Journal* (1799) stated that attacks were normally conducted in echelon of squadrons, the leading squadron attracting the enemy's fire, with those following (at 150-yard intervals) falling upon the enemy before he had time to reload, and altering course slightly to strike the enemy a little way one side or other of the initial breach made by the leading squadron. Attack in echelon exemplified the advantage of mounting a charge in waves, the second to exploit the success of the first or to renew the assault if the first had been driven away.

Squadron action must to a degree have decreased the ability of a regimental commander to retain complete control. The experience of

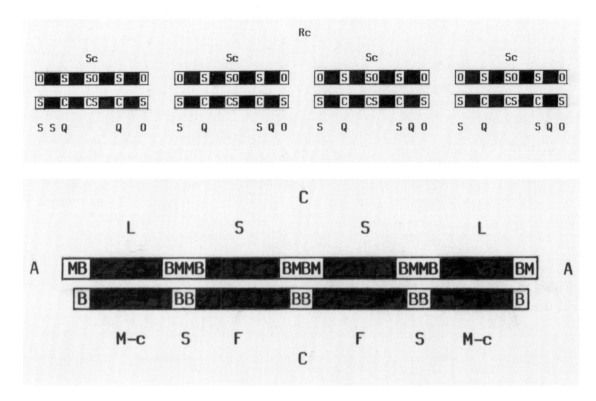

Above: A typical deployment: a squadron or French light cavalry in line, as it might be for action, showing the disposition or officers and NCOs within the two ranks (solid black), and to front and rear. Key:

A *Adjutant-major (senior sergeant-major)*

B *Brigadier (corporal)*

C *captain*

F *Fourrier (quartermaster-corporal)*

L *lieutenant*

M *Maréchal-des-Logis (sergeant)*

M-c *Maréchal-des-Logis Chef (sergeant-major)*

S *Sous-lieutenant (junior lieutenant)*

Frederick Ponsonby at Waterloo must have been typical: shortly before he received his celebrated injuries, he remarked to a subordinate, 'Hang it, what can detain our centre squadron? I must get back and see ...'[79] Alternatively, the ability of squadron commanders to exercise a degree of independent command must have been advantageous at times: for example, the famous success of the King's German Legion at Garcia Hernandez was instigated by the squadron-commanders Captains Augustus von Reizenstein and Gustavus von der Decken, rather than by the brigade-commander Major-General Eberhardt von Bock. (He was too short-sighted to see the enemy, and charged off with his leading squadron in another direction; von Reizenstein and von der Decken had their squadrons in echelon behind the leading element, and were thus able to select another target for their attack, further evidence of the flexibility of the echelon formation.)

Although it was generally believed that the line was the best formation for the charge, opinions conflicted as to whether two or three ranks were the most efficient. (Distinction should always be made over the terms 'line' and 'rank': ranks described the deployment of the sub-unit – troop or squadron – and 'lines' the larger formation. 'Two lines' would normally

Chasseurs à Cheval of Napoleon's Imperial Guard, in petite tenue (undress uniform, left) and full dress (right); the mounted trooper carries his carbine slung from the spring-clip on his shoulder-belt. (Print by Montigneul after Eugène Lami).

imply two rows of regiments or squadrons, arrayed in line one behind the other, irrespective of whether the units in question were formed in two or three ranks). Supporters of the three-rank line included Warnery, who advocated the two-rank line only when a unit could not otherwise match the frontage of the opponent, to prevent the enemy overlapping. He recommended three ranks, because 'a smaller number of ranks would not have sufficient strength nor weight, and would not be enabled to furnish the shock in charging: whereas in three deep the two rear ranks not only press the first forward, but prevent them from stopping, and any of the troopers retiring ... A squadron formed in two ranks is very subject to wavering, and much easier broken than one of three, which must also naturally have a greater weight in the shock, and be much more difficult for an enemy to penetrate.'[80]

Nevertheless, the two-rank line was more common. It was, for example, decreed by the Russian regulations of 1796, which noted that the third rank served only to impede movement and was dangerous when a horse fell in the first rank, a point emphasised by Marmont when he commented that the two-rank line was the best to minimise disruption in such a case, and that three ranks were only productive of confusion in action. The Austrian regulations of 1784 preserved the old three-rank line, but they were revised successively, and earlier practice, specified in 1804 and confirmed by a new issue in 1806, decreed the two-rank line as the standard formation. This, in fact, was fairly standard throughout most armies; as the British regulations stated, 'The *troop* and the squadron are formed two deep',[81] though some advocated a variation according to the target of an attack. For example, a writer in the *British Military Library or Journal* advocated three or even four ranks for a charge against cavalry, when there would be no musketry to bring down horses in the first rank and thus disorder the remainder. The 1796 Prussian regulations did, in fact, specify a three-rank line for the attack, but the third was not intended directly to follow the first two, but to form into two bodies, one behind each wing, to swing wide of the line and engage the enemy flanks if opportunity arose, and a similar flank-reserve was also specified by the 1812 regulations. Flank-protection during a charge was included in the regulations of several armies; Austrian cavalry, for example, was instructed to use flank-guards during a charge, and although in 1812 the carbine was largely withdrawn from the Russian cavalry (generally reissued in 1814), sixteen 'flankers' per squadron retained them and were ordered to fan out to protect the flanks of a charge.

When attacking in line, it was essential that intervals be left, for example between troops or squadrons, to permit a defeated first line, or retiring skirmishers, to retire directly to the rear without disordering the lines following.

Despite different national procedures, the cardinal rules of successful cavalry charges were universal. Discipline at all stages was held to be essential (though in practice the reverse was often the case). One commentator noted: 'To obtain what are called *good fighting lines* quickly, and to advance and retire with steadiness, and without losing that compactness which is the chief essential of cavalry, must always be the main object';[82] and it was also remarked that the less officers shifted their position, the more order was preserved and the quicker manoeuvres could be performed. The importance of clear orders was paramount, as the British regulations noted: 'All commands must be given by officers, firm, loud, and explicit; every officer must therefore be accustomed to give such commands, even to the smallest bodies, in the full extent of his voice; by such bodies he must not only be heard, but by the leaders of others who are dependent upon his motions.' It was fortunate that orders for the charge *could* be given concisely – once formed in line no more than 'March!' – 'Trot!' – 'Gallop!' – 'Charge!',[83] as the process could be considerably more complicated for manoeuvres normally executed in situations not quite so hazardous; for example, when a regiment in line changed its face by pivoting on the central squadron, some thirty-five verbal commands were specified.

Before a charge was commenced, reconnaissance was necessary, not only of the terrain but to identify both the target of the charge, and its precise location, to ensure correct timing, which was paramount to enable the charge to strike its target with maximum impetus. The charge might also involve the initial advance being preceded by skirmishers, who would move out of the way before it reached its full speed. The essence of a charge was described effectively by the British regulations:

> Whatever distance the squadron has to go over, it may move at a brisk trot till within two hundred and fifty yards of the enemy, and then gallop. The word CHARGE! is given when within eighty yards, and the gallop increased as much as the body can bear in good order... At the instant of the shock, the body must be well back; the horse not restrained by the bitt, but determined forward by the spur: rising in the stirrups, and pointing the sword, will always occasion a shake in the squadron; it will naturally be done when necessary. It is in the uniform velocity of the squadron, that its effect consists; the spur as much as the sword tends to overset an opposite enemy; when one has nearly accomplished this end, the other may compleat [*sic*] it ... In the walk the sword is carried with the blade resting on the right arm. In the trot and gallop the right hand must be steadied on the right thigh, the point of the sword rather inclining forward – and in the CHARGE the hand is lifted, and the sword carried rather forward

Chasseurs à Cheval of Napoleon's Imperial Guard: a kettledrummer wearing oriental-style costume, and a member of the Young Guard element of the Chasseurs, which wore shakos instead of the more usual fur busby. (Print by Lacoste after Demoraine.)

and crossways across the head, with the edge outwards. The regiments and squadrons must be well dressed before they move; horses perfectly straight, and carried on so during the whole attack; files on no account crowding; paces even and determined; horses in hand, and perfect steadiness and attention of every individual.[84]

Similar tactics seem to have been quite general; the Austrian regulations, for example, stressed the need to preserve a regulated pace, with the gallop being restrained so as not to exhaust the horses before full speed was attained in the last eighty paces before contact, at which point the trumpeters sounded 'Alarm!', officers called '*Marsch! Marsch!* ', and the troops raised their sabres above their heads.

Great emphasis was placed on the need to maintain strict discipline at this stage of the charge, hence the above reference to speed being restricted to 'as much as the body can bear in good order'. Wellington commented that if the pace at which cavalry manoeuvred were too rapid, the looseness of the files was likely to cause confusion, and 'the horses are jaded before the moment of exertion arrives'. When that moment came, the tendency was for the cavalry to 'become unmanageable in proportion as [the] rate of going is increased; and this is another reason for shortening the pace in all movements, excepting the last and decisive charge'. He also stated that care should be taken that commands should only be given by those authorised by regulation (as repetition of orders by subordinates tended to cause confusion), and 'to keep the charge, as well as all other movements, at a pace with which, at least, the middling goers, if not the slowest, can keep up'. 'It is impossible to preserve order, and go quick in large bodies. It is equally so to traverse the spaces which the manoeuvre of large bodies requires should be traversed, and keep the horse in a state to do any thing, if the pace is not slow. But the great object of all in the cavalry, and particularly in that of the line, is order ...'[85]

These statements were qualified by others; Marmont, for example, was less concerned with the preservation of the *closest* order than with the ability to manoeuvre at speed in reasonable formation, believing that it was worth sacrificing some degree of order for impetus, without which a charge would not be likely to succeed, provided that the troops were trained to obey the order to rally immediately, so that the apparent disorder of a charge would not adversely affect the ability to re-form.

One factor which could disrupt a charge was a tendency for horses to crush in towards the centre, which became worse as the formation increased in size. Lewis Edward Nolan, the cavalry expert and tactical writer who gained his greatest but most dubious fame as the bearer of the order to advance the Light Brigade at Balaklava, wrote that he had ridden in formations in the Austrian cavalry when the 'crush' was so great that his horse had been lifted off its legs, causing great pain to the rider, and that attempts to remedy this not only resulted in the closure of the necessary gaps in an advancing line, but rendered it disorganised and vulnerable to attack. Considerable injury could be done by this crush; Warnery wrote of the bruises which could be sustained from the knees, carbines and scabbards of adjoining troopers, and advocated that long boots with stiff tops should be used to permit cavalry 'to charge closer in line, than they have ever been able to do since suple [*sic*] boots has [*sic*] been adopted'.[86] These were like the long boots worn by the French heavy cavalry regiments whose principal duty was the knee-to-knee charge, although they were very restricting when dismounted, as noted in the Eckmühl anecdote included in

Trumpeters in cuirassier regiments were not normally equipped with the cuirass, perhaps a relic of their original non-combatant status: trumpeter of the French 7th Cuirassiers. (Print by Martinet.)

the section on armour. The injuries which could be sustained by this crush could be severe; for example, even in a field day in Hyde Park in 1794, a Life Guard 'had his thigh broke, by being jammed between his own horse and that of his comrade'.[87]

The consequences of a charge were different according to whether the target was cavalry or infantry. When bodies of cavalry were opposed to each other, generally one seems to have wavered and broken formation before contact, so that a mêlée could occur. An Austrian writer stated that if cavalry charged in close formation, they could never penetrate an enemy which held its own close order, envisaging the absurd sight of opposing horses banging their noses together, with their riders unable to reach forward sufficiently to strike at the enemy. What seems to have happened in many cases was as described by another commentator, who remarked that two lines of cavalry would rarely come into contact while keeping their order so perfectly as to fight in line: 'one or other must either give way, turn about, and fly, or else, falling into disorder, be penetrated and passed through, so as to produce a complete mêlée, in which the party that first regains any

Austrian heavy cavalry, c. 1813: the cuirassiers in the foreground wear the cuirass with front-plate only; the dragoon (left) can be seen to carry his ramrod attached to a shoulder-belt. The full campaign equipment depicted includes bundles of forage carried upon the saddle. (Print after J.A. Klein.)

degree of order, will have the instant advantage. This is the moment when the *arme blanche* ... really comes into play, and by no means in the act of charging, when the strength of the horse's legs has a far greater effect than the vigour of the rider's arm.'[88]

Clearly, the morale consideration was paramount, exemplified by William Tomkinson's description of a fight near Fuentes de Oñoro in May 1811, in which a squadron of 16th Light Dragoons was cut-up by a French force: 'This is the only instance I ever met with of two bodies of cavalry coming in

A charge by Austrian cuirassiers, 1796. (Print after R. von Ottenfeld.)

opposition, and both standing, as invariably, as I have observed it, one or the other runs away.'[89] It must have taken troops of some nerve to face a well-ordered charge without flinching, but despite Tomkinson's opinion there are many accounts of this happening. Alternatively, some combats must have resembled an exercise held in Paris during the Allied occupation, before the Tsar and other dignitaries, the effect of which was presumably the more striking as it involved a situation in which neither side could expect to be hurt. In demonstrating an attack, a body of British heavy cavalry approached some Brunswick cavalry:

> They came on at first steadily, covered by skirmishers; by-and-by they formed line, and the trumpets sounded to trot. Then came the signal to gallop, and to charge; and it was obeyed with such a show of vigour, as fairly to upset the common sense of the Brunswickers. A panic seized them: they imagined that they were going to be ridden down; and suddenly wheeling round, they scampered off in all directions, making a way for themselves, without respect of persons,

through the very middle of the crowd. I defy a stoic to retain his gravity, if he had witnessed the scenes that followed. There were people shrieking and running for their lives: there the Brunswickers spurring as if a legion of fiends had been in pursuit of them, and casting over their shoulders, from time to time, looks of the most abject terror. And, finally, there was the heavy brigade, grave as judges, till the trumpet sounded a halt, when, as if an irresistible impulse had come on them, they all burst into a roar of laughter. I never saw such a scene of mirth as that parade ground presented; and unless my memory deceive me, among the heartiest laughers of all, were the Duke himself, and the Emperor of Russia.[90]

It is possible that such a fate might befall *any* cavalry, according to circumstances. Wellington seems to have suggested this:

The unwieldy nature of the lance for close-quarter combat is exemplified in this portrayal of an incident at Albuera, in which Marshal William Beresford disarmed a lancer who attacked him. Note the lancer's pistol attached to the clip of his shoulder-belt. (Engraving by T. Sutherland after William Heath.)

Few troops will bear a surprise and a general panic; and at all events young cavalry are much more easily affected by these circumstances, and the effect upon them is much more extensive and more sensibly felt ... than similar circumstances operating upon infantry in the same state of discipline. Their horses afford them means of flight, and when once cavalry lose their order it is impossible to restore it. For this reason I am always inclined to keep the cavalry out of action, as long as possible.[91]

Marmont confirmed that in cavalry combat it was usual for one side to falter and turn about, and that consequently morale was of crucial significance. This seems to have been recognised generally and influenced the actions of troopers as they charged; de Brack, for example, advocated that swords be drawn only shortly before contact, which together with the action of standing in the stirrups and shouting would not only undermine the morale of the enemy but would hearten the attackers.

Despite the criticisms of cavalry firearms, and the acknowledgement that they were only intended for skirmishing, there were cases in which they were used in more general fighting. The French cavalry in particular on occasion seem to have relied on meeting incoming charges with carbine-fire from horseback, despite a well-known maxim that to meet a charge at the halt was to invite disaster. An incidence of the tactic having some success was at Eylau, when the 20th *Chasseurs à Cheval* were attacked by a strong force of dragoons, whose pace had been slowed to a walk by the soft ground and the snow upon it. The 20th's Colonel Castex (described by Marbot as 'an excellent man'[92]) checked that his men had loaded, then ordered the officers into the line (presumably from positions in front) and delivered a volley at the oncoming Russians at close range, which devastated their front rank. The two forces then engaged with sabres. It is likely that in this case, carbine-fire had been used because of the state of the ground, over which neither side could manage even a trot.

Under more usual conditions, meeting a charge with fire was a more hazardous undertaking, as the impetus was all on the side of the attackers. At Ostrovno, for example, the French 16th *Chasseurs à Cheval* tried to repel a Russian attack by firing at them at thirty yards' range, but were overthrown when the fire failed to stop the incoming charge. Another incident occurred at Sahagun, when the French 8th Dragoons and 1st Provisional *Chasseurs à Cheval* engaged the British 15th Hussars. The French regiments formed in line, one behind the other, making a body six deep, and began to fire even before the British had wheeled into line. The French appear not to have begun to move as the 15th charged, but continued to shoot – evidently with little effect – and were overturned when the British charge went in. 'The shock was terrible; horses and men were overthrown, and a shriek of terror, intermixed with oaths, groans, and prayers for mercy, issued from the whole extent of their front. Our men, though surprised at the depth of the ranks, pressed forward until they had cut their way quite through.'[93]

Carbine-fire could even be delivered by cavalry which was advancing, and not just by skirmishers. For example, at Alteglofsheim, following the battle of Eckmühl, when advancing at a walk towards a large force of Austrian cavalry, Nansouty's French heavy cavalry halted to permit the carabiniers in the centre of his line to fire a volley at about 100 yards, before the formation was ordered to trot, the pace at which they met the Austrians riding at them at full gallop.

As mentioned above, despite some accounts of cavalry remaining static to meet a charge (probably in most cases under unusual circumstances), it was generally held that it was courting disaster to receive a charge at the halt. The British regulations made the point forcibly: 'There are many occasions in war, where with advantage, from the nature of their arms and other circumstances, infantry can and ought to await the attack; yet there are hardly any where it can be eligible for cavalry to receive it: though circumstance of situation may prevent a line from advancing much, it should

Cavalry combat: the cut and guard depicted in this illustration of Corporal Logan of the British 13th Light Dragoons about to kill Colonel Chamorin of the French 26th Dragoons at Campo Mayor. (Print by M. Dubourg after Denis Dighton.)

never absolutely stand still to receive the shock, otherwise its defeat is inevitable.'[94]

The popular conception of the cavalry charge, its speed building up until the horsemen were riding *à outrance* (a flat-out gallop), was not always what actually happened. Rapid movement was certainly a great advantage, but only, as Marmont admitted, provided sufficient order were retained. In some cases, however, order might be sacrificed for speed and not be condemned. Commenting on a sortie from Nijmegen in November 1794, for example, the *British Military Library or Journal* noted that although the commanding general, 'a foreigner, was exasperated at the quickness and irregularity of the charge' of the British 15th Light Dragoons, it advised that 'when infantry are flying in all directions', for cavalry to maintain 'form or exactness' (other than the maintenance of a reserve) 'may lose them the opportunity of doing material mischief to their enemies'.[95]

Although what Wellington termed 'galloping at everything' is often quoted as a failing of the British cavalry, the sacrifice of order for speed was by no means peculiar to them. One large operation in which the cardinal rules were not followed was the cavalry attack at Wachau, near Leipzig, in which Murat led a successful charge which overran an Allied battery and captured twenty-six guns. Saxon cuirassiers held this ground and began to try to remove the artillery, but the remainder of the French horsemen charged on, without being rallied and without keeping an adequate reserve to cover their retreat. Including some inexperienced troopers (most charges seem to have been executed in column, for example), on horses not in prime condition from previous hard service, the disorganised mass was unable to resist the Allied counterattack, which drove on and retook almost all the lost guns, negating the earlier success which might have been consolidated had not Murat been quite so impetuous. In fairness, though, it would be unreasonable to lay all blame for such events upon officers or commanding generals: even among disciplined cavalry it was remarked that at times it was impossible to stop the mounts getting out of control and careering onwards too rapidly.

On other occasions, a 'charge' might be delivered at a much slower pace even than a 'slow gallop'. It seems, for example, that in many cases heavy cavalry deliberately moved at a reduced pace: besides the slower speed helping to retain order, horses loaded with the weight of a cuirassier might

Cavalry combat: the famous British pugilist John Shaw, who was killed as a member of the 2nd Life Guards at Waterloo, depicted here engaging two French cuirassiers. (Print published by Thomas Kelly.)

not be able to move very fast for any great distance. Some commanders regarded this as a disadvantage, but others claimed it more intimidating to the enemy and recommended that cuirassiers only gallop when pursuing a defeated opponent. Jomini advocated a fast trot (to ensure preservation of order), but others quoted examples such as the French losses sustained at Aspern-Essling as being due to the same thing. When both sides adopted this practice (as was reported at Friedland, for example), they might trot, or even walk up to each other, in which case the chance of a prolonged mêlée was perhaps more likely, as neither would be upset by the other's speed, nor sufficiently intimidated to be on the point of breaking before contact was made. Other factors which might prevent a charge from gathering much speed were the configuration of the terrain and the proximity of the enemy. For example, a witness of one of the most celebrated charges of the period, that of the Royal Scots Greys at Waterloo, described how different it was from the attack *à outrance* depicted in Lady Butler's famous painting of the incident, *Scotland for Ever*. In reality, the regiment came over the crest of the Mont St-Jean ridge, passed through their own infantry, and almost immediately ran into the advancing French, so that they 'actually walked over this Column'.[96]

Cavalry upon tired horses might make charges subsequent to their first at no more than a trot – this was observed, for example, at Waterloo – and heavy ground might make any rapid speed quite impossible. That the nature of the terrain might neutralise the effect of cavalry was exemplified by an incident at Dresden, in which General Bourdesoule's French cuirassier division approached an Austrian infantry brigade. There occurred a fairly unusual conversation between the opposing commanders when Bourdesoule called upon the Austrians to surrender, as the day was so wet that the infantry's muskets wouldn't fire. The Austrian retorted that the ground was so heavy that the cavalry was up to its hocks, and thus unable to charge. Bourdesoule said he would bring up guns, which the Austrian refused to believe because of the difficulty of hauling through the mud; but the French horse artillery had been allocated additional team-horses to overcome this problem, and at the sight of a battery unlimbering at thirty yards' range, the Austrian surrendered. This also recalls the fact that it was advisable to accompany cavalry with horse artillery whenever possible; but it is noteworthy that many of the most celebrated charges were made without this asset.

When opposing cavalry formations came into contact, violent hand-to-hand combat might ensue, though de Gonneville noted that sword-fights 'only come within the duty of a cavalry officer in the most minute proportion' of his service.[97] He quoted an experience of his at Saguntum, where he attacked a Spanish lancer; having parried a lance-thrust, he ran his opponent through the body. Because this was a single combat and took place in full view of his unit, news of it spread far and wide and was still being talked about twenty-two years later, suggesting that such events were somewhat uncommon. Nevertheless, actions could be contested most fiercely, to the extent that James Smithies of the British Royal Dragoons recalled how at Waterloo some of the combatants grabbed one another and grappled like wrestlers. Accounts exist of some of the opposing ranks opening, where they could, to allow the combatants to ride past each other, slashing as they went, and indeed such actions usually turned into somewhat confused mêlées which ended when one side withdrew, so that

Cavalry on the battlefield: French dragoons advance at Aldenhoven (2 October 1794). (Print after Mozin.)

the majority of casualties might occur as the victors began the pursuit, when the fight could be spread over a very wide area. One such action was described by an eyewitness of the fight at Campo Mayor:

> The French manoeuvred most beautifully ... and sustained three charges of our cavalry without breaking ... I saw so many instances of individual bravery, as raised my opinion of mankind in general many degrees. The French certainly are fine and brave soldiers, but the superiority of our English horses, and more particularly the superiority of swordsmanship our fellows showed, decided every contest in our favour; it was absolutely like a game at *prison bars*, which you must have seen at school, except the three charges. The whole way across the plain was a succession of individual contests, here and there, as the cavalry all dispersed.[98]

At this stage of an action, two features became absolutely paramount: the need to keep a reserve and to have discipline sufficient to rally those who had been engaged, whether victorious or not. It was at this stage that even victorious troops were at their most vulnerable to counterattack: horses tired, the unit scattered over perhaps a wide area, the men possibly confused after violent conflict, officers and NCOs not always on hand to give the necessary commands. With fully disciplined cavalry, units which had charged could rally quickly and renew the assault, or if in the enemy's rear, charge back to safety. There are many examples of Napoleon's cavalry, for example, making charge after charge and continuing to rally after each, thus remaining an effective (if diminishing and tiring) asset to their commander, and in so doing demonstrating impressive standards of determination, morale and discipline.

The necessity of keeping troops in hand, acting as a reserve, could similarly hardly be underestimated; such troops were essential, either to exploit a victory or to cover the withdrawal of a defeated attack. If no reserve were held back, or if the reserve became involved in the main charge, disaster could ensue. This was by no means inevitable: some successful charges were conducted without the maintenance of a reserve, or with the reserve too far away to be effective; but a graphic example of what could occur was provided by the first great charge of the British heavy cavalry at Waterloo. The Household Brigade's charge was successful, with one regiment (Royal Horse Guards) remaining in reserve to cover the withdrawal of the others; but the Union Brigade came to grief, at least in part because the regiment ordered to stay back as a reserve (by no less than the army's overall cavalry commander, the Earl of Uxbridge), the 2nd Dragoons (Royal Scots Greys), took part in the charge instead.

> The joint failings of not keeping a reserve, and of not rallying once the enemy had been put to flight, were demonstrated on a number of occasions when British charges got out of hand. In general the British cavalry was much more competent than these few instances would suggest, but nevertheless they formed salutary lessons applicable to all cavalry, of whatever nationality. The British regulations were clear enough: 'When the shock of the squadron has broken the order of the opposite enemy, part may be ordered to pursue and keep up the advantage; but its great object is instantly to rally and renew its efforts in a body ... if ... itself put in disorder or confusion, it must retire as well as it can, to make way for those that support it, and must rally as soon as possible under the protection of others. A squadron should never be so hurried, as to bring up the horses blown to the charge.'[99] In the event, however, much of this seems to have been ignored in training, and had to be learned when on campaign. William Tomkinson criticised the practice of 'each regiment estimating its merit by the celerity of movement ... we do everything so quickly that it is impossible men can understand what they are about ... Before the enemy, except in charging, I never saw troops go beyond a trot ... In England I never saw nor heard of cavalry taught to charge, disperse, and form, which, if I only taught a regiment one thing, I think it should be that.'[100]

The need to rally – and even to keep a reserve – did depend upon circumstances, being of less importance if the fight were over and no enemy troops were threatening, or when involving only small bodies of cavalry. The author of the above criticism himself recalled an example of how he disregarded these cardinal rules. At Llerena he was urging on his men when his commander, Le Marchant himself, ordered him to rally after a successful charge. 'He said, "Halt, and form your men." I said, "The enemy are in greater confusion." "You must halt." "Must I call out, 'Halt'?" I asked. Seeing the general hesitate (he would not give the order), I called to the men to come on, and we drove the enemy a mile, in the greatest confusion.'[101] Indeed, the act of rallying men under such circumstances was often very difficult: 'Having rode together nearly a mile, pell-mell, cutting and slashing each other, the men were quite wild and the horses blown',[102] as one described. The exhilaration of victory in such circumstances might be too much to resist even for units which in other respects might be regarded as well trained and fully disciplined.

The importance of discipline in cavalry operations was exemplified by Napoleon when comparing individual and collective skill. He remarked that although two Mamelukes, individually superbly skilled, could outfight three Frenchmen, 300 Frenchmen could defeat an equal body of Mamelukes, and 1,000 Frenchmen would beat 1,500 Mamelukes. Wellington used a very similar analogy: 'I considered our cavalry so inferior to the French from want of order, although I consider one squadron a match for two French squadrons, that I should not have liked to see four British squadrons opposed to four French; and, as the numbers increased, and order of course became more necessary, I was more unwilling to risk our cavalry without having a great superiority of numbers.' Napoleon's heavy cavalry, he said, could be used to occupy parts of the enemy's position, and hold the position until the infantry could relieve them; 'This shows the difference of his principles and mine; but it was to be attributed to his having his cavalry in order. Mine would gallop, but could not preserve their order.'[103]

Following the débâcle at Maguilla, Wellington expounded his ideas:

It is occasioned entirely by the trick our officers of cavalry have acquired of galloping at every thing, and their galloping back as fast as they gallop on the enemy. They never consider their situation, and never think of manoeuvring before an enemy – so little that one would think they cannot manoeuvre, excepting on Wimbledon Common: and when they use their arm as it ought to be used, viz., offensively, they never keep nor provide for a reserve. All cavalry should charge in two lines, of which one should be in reserve; if obliged to charge in one line, at least one-third, should be ordered beforehand to pull up, and form in second line, as soon as the charge should be given, and the enemy has been broken and retired.[104]

The reason for the incapacity of some officers, he stated, was partly the complexity of cavalry service when compared with that of the infantry:

To understand it well is much more difficult [and] their minds have never been fairly brought to the contemplation of the true principles on which the cavalry service should be conducted. Let them once understand that the undue celerity of the movements, that dust and confusion go for nothing, and are injurious to their prescribed utility and regulation, and they will very soon be as useful in their line of service as the officers of infantry are in theirs.[105]

Finally, after the experience of the Union Brigade at Waterloo in particular, Wellington issued detailed orders to brigade-commanders, which summarise the essence of successful cavalry service of any nationality. He stated that the maintenance of a reserve was essential, never less than half and even up to two-thirds of the strength. Cavalry should deploy in three bodies, the first two in line and the reserve in column, but able to move rapidly into line. When facing enemy cavalry, the three bodies should be 400–500 yards behind one another, a space sufficient for a defeated first line to retire without disordering the second, but close enough for the second line to lend support; but against infantry, the second line should be only 200 yards in the rear, so as to be able to make a charge before the infantry had time to recover from that of the first line. Finally, when the first line charged, the supports should follow at a walk, so as not to become carried away or involved in the mêlée and thus lose formation or control.

Emphasis was put upon the necessity of executing a charge at the most opportune moment, for example so as to fall upon the enemy's flank, while he was deploying, or upon troops who were already wavering; and at the correct distance, to maximise the 'shock' effect. The results of a charge made at just the right moment could be devastating. An example was Schwarzenberg's charge at Le Cateau–Cambresis (or Beaumont) in April 1794, when using folds in the terrain as cover he attacked in three successive lines and overturned the large French force which was threatening to raise the siege of Landrecies. A similarly decisive action was Kellermann's greatest charge at Marengo, which seconded Desaix's advance and helped salvage a victory from near defeat. Executed with perfect timing, it overthrew the advancing Austrian column in moments, as suggested by his own account of the action: 'The Austrians advanced to follow up their success, in all the disorder and security of victory. I see it; I am in the midst of them; they lay down their arms. The whole did not occupy so much time as it has taken me to write these six lines.'[106] That this feat was performed with cavalry already tired from heroic exertions earlier in the day demonstrates the resilience which is recorded in many accounts.

One of the most famous of Napoleon's cavalry commanders, immortalised by his decisive charge at Marengo: François-Etienne, comte de Kellermann (1770–1835), who succeeded to the title of duc de Valmy upon the death of his distinguished father in 1820.

Equally, some charges seem to have been ill-timed, although the commanders were not necessarily culpable, as two incidents from Waterloo seem to demonstrate. One of the most trying experiences for cavalry was surely that of sitting immobile under fire, awaiting orders and unable to strike back. Not all were as stalwart as General Louis Lepic, who when under terrible fire at Eylau called to his *Grenadiers à Cheval* of Napoleon's Imperial Guard, '*Haut les têtes! La mitraille n'est pas de la merde!*' ('Heads up! Those are bullets, not turds!'[107]) A similar ordeal was endured by French cavalry at Waterloo, and it was said that when questioned about the timing of the subsequent great charges (made largely without the support which would have given them a chance of success), General Samuel l'Héritier (commander of the 11th Cavalry Division) mentioned this as one factor. They were positioned in such a way as to be exposed to a fire so galling 'that the impetuosity of the French character would no longer be restrained within bounds ... and there arose such a dangerous clamour in the ranks, and such earnest demands to be led forward, and in their own words, to have "*vie pour vie*" [a life for a life], that the officers were compelled to lay aside their better discretion, and at once bring them into action at all hazards'.[108]

If de Brack is to be believed, at least one charge at Waterloo was launched by accident. Watching the battle, he recalled that he exclaimed the enemy was lost, whereupon some officers of cavalry rode up to him to see for themselves; their troops began to edge forward behind them and, seeing the movement, an adjoining unit presumed it had to follow the other cavalry which was already charging, and so the Guard cavalry seconded the attack, without orders.[109] Against such examples of dangerous ardour, there are also accounts of cavalry being positively unwilling to engage an enemy (perhaps not surprisingly!) Personal accounts and opinions should always be evaluated with some circumspection, but – to take Waterloo again as an example – the account of the battle by Horace Churchill (ADC to Lord Hill) compared the exceptional heroism of Napoleon's cavalry with what he thought was the opposite on the part of the British cavalry (with some exceptions). Though markedly different from other accounts, it is worth noting that Churchill claimed to have observed extreme reticence to engage on the part of some cavalry, to the extent that he claimed that the cavalry commander, the Earl of Uxbridge, when riding over to the Foot Guards remarked to them that he was glad to be among men who did not make him ashamed to be English![110]

Against infantry, cavalry often varied its mode of operation; the *British Military Library or Journal*, for example, recommended that against squares, attacks should be made simultaneously against a face and at least one corner, in waves 150 yards apart, with thirty-yard gaps in the succeeding waves to permit the first waves to retire without disordering those who followed. By attacking in echelon of squadrons, it was thought that the infantry would not have time to reload before the second wave was upon them, unless they had the composure to reserve their fire until actually attacked, and then only fire by platoons; 'But,' the article noted with much accuracy, 'where is the infantry which ever acted with so much countenance on the day of battle?'[111]

It was held generally that squares – rectangular formations of three or four ranks of infantry, facing outwards and with levelled bayonets – were impervious to cavalry attack, unless the cavalry were accompanied by artillery (to which squares were terribly vulnerable) or unless, as mentioned previously, the infantry were unable to fire because of wet weather. Some theorists, however, believed that cavalry *could* break squares if only they had sufficient nerve, opinions which seem to diverge markedly from what actually occurred. For example, in his work on cavalry tactics Count Bismarck stated that if determined, cavalry must prevail. The British tactical writer John Mitchell was another, claiming that even thirty horsemen should have been able to overthrow 'a moderate battalion of infantry … for surely no one can well maintain with ordinary gravity, that the bayonets of the kneeling ranks form a barrier capable of arresting by its consistency a body of determined horsemen arriving at full speed against them, so that whatever might be the loss of the leading assailants, the boasted formation would at least be thrown open, and the crowded and helpless mass of defenders exposed without any means of resistance to the hoofs and sabres of the succeeding centaurs'.[112]

Instead, cavalry in such situations usually edged away to right or left of the point attacked, and were thus exposed to more musketry than had they charged home, presuming that their mounts *could* have been impelled on to the very bayonets of the square. Some very unfair criticism was made of the French cavalry for declining to throw itself on to the squares at Waterloo, 'proof of professional ignorance or insufficiency of courage; for there is a sort of three-quarter courage ... that will gallop up to the bayonet, and even bravado round the squares, and yet wants the resolution to dash, at less ultimate risk, perhaps, into the midst of levelled muskets and presented bayonets; but those who cannot set an example of such resolution have no business on horseback'.[113] Another account noted:

> Not in a single instance did they preserve their order and come in a compact body against the ridge of bayonets; and even the best of those charges ... failed at a considerable distance from the infantry. The horsemen opened out and hedged away from every volley. Sometimes they even halted and turned before they had been fired at; sometimes, after receiving the fire of the standing ranks only. In this manner they flew from one square to another, receiving the fire of different squares as they passed; they flew (more frequently at a trot, however, than at a gallop) from one side of the square to another, and flourished their sabres; individuals, and small parties, here and there rode up close to the ranks. It is said that on some points they actually cut at the bayonets with their swords and fired their pistols at the officers.[114]

Nevertheless, the efforts made by the French cavalry at Waterloo impressed almost all who witnessed them, though without artillery support their charges were futile as long as the squares remained firm. Cavalrymen realised that irrespective of their own courage, it was an unusual horse which would charge ahead without flinching:

> When he is urged against the terrible face of the infantry square, more resembling a living volcano than any phalanx of human invention, when his sight is obscured by clouds of rolling smoke, only broken by the quick flash of the musket and the occasional gleam of the bayonet, the animal becomes bewildered with terror, and wheeling round, in spite of rein and spur, rushes from the unequal conflict, where he seems to know almost by instinct that his destruction is instant and inevitable. Let any one, officer or soldier, who has ever charged a square, deny, if he can, the truth of this picture.[115]

The charge: French 4th Hussars. (Print after Detaille).

Another witness recalled how the cavalry stood some forty yards from the squares, unable to advance, unwilling to retire, and as fast as they were shot others moved up to replace them. It was so obvious that these brave attacks could not succeed that some British troops remarked, 'Here come those damned fools again!',[116] and seeming to realise the futility of their task, Lieutenant James Mill recalled, that all the French could do was snarl, 'fierce gesticulations and angry scowls, in which a display of incisors became very apparent to all'. So marked was this that eventually the British officers ordered their men to reply in kind, ordering as each charge approached, 'Now men, make faces'![117]

The crucial consideration about attacking a square was the resolution of the infantry, who were secure so long as they kept their nerve and order; as William Tomkinson remarked, breaking a square by cavalry alone was 'a thing never heard of. The infantry either break before the cavalry come close up, or they drive them back with their fire.'[118] Nevertheless, there

A trooper of the Gendarmerie d'Elite (left) and a sapeur (pioneer) of the Grenadiers à Pied of the French Imperial Guard, the former showing the method of carrying the carbine muzzle-down, in a tubular 'bucket' attached to the saddle. (Engraving by Moraine.)

were occasions when the cavalry *did* break squares, though usually under peculiar circumstances (such as the examples quoted earlier, of lances or pistols being used to breach a square where muskets had been rendered useless by rain). If the cavalry operated in conjunction with artillery or infantry there was a far greater chance of success, but much still depended upon the resolution of the troops attacked. This was a critical factor in perhaps the most celebrated case of the breaking of squares by unsupported cavalry, at Garcia Hernandez in July 1812, when dragoons of the King's German Legion engaged French infantry of Foy's 1st Division, which must have been tired from marching for well over a week without much rest (including forty-two miles in one day), probably with scanty supplies and no reserve of ammunition, and perhaps dispirited by the defeat at Salamanca the preceding day. The dragoons attacked uphill in echelon of squadrons, against heavy musketry, but the French were retiring in column and appear to have formed 'solid squares' by facing the ranks outwards, rather than the more effective hollow square. The initial attack was made perhaps with little hope of success, until a horse was brought down and fell *upon* one face of the square, crushing the men beneath it, and into this gap other troopers rushed. As they began to cut at the infantry, a remarkable thing happened: the formation dissolved, about fifty ran away, and the rest grounded their arms in a gesture of surrender.

The following squadron made for another retreating body of infantry, which seems to have faced-about and fired, but must have been disheartened by what had befallen their comrades, and it is unclear whether a proper square was ever formed. Men began to break and run before the cavalry even got among them, and they were scattered; and a third 'square' was also ridden down (which some state was composed of those who had escaped from the earlier fighting, in which case their morale must have been greatly shaken). Only when the cavalry was 'blown' and disordered did a fourth square drive them back. Although Tomkinson described it as 'one of the best charges ever made'[119] and the French general, Maximilien Foy, as the most daring cavalry charge of the entire war, it also seems to demonstrate the vulnerability of unsteady squares. One commentator asserted that the French were 'retiring without much order, and formed hastily into squares of the worst description',[120] and apart from exhaustion, Foy's men may well have been short of

French Chasseur à Cheval, 1812, showing the common practice of carrying the cloak rolled over one shoulder, as a rudimentary protection against sword-cuts. (Engraving by Best & Leloire after Hippolyte Bellangé.)

ammunition, as some were certainly reduced to throwing stones at the cavalry (though this may have been done by men who had dropped their muskets to escape the first charge). A further factor was the resolution of the cavalry, which according to one of them was exceptional, the men thirsting for an opportunity to wreak upon the French 'the bloody revenge that we have so long owed them'[121] for having occupied their Hanoverian homeland.

No surprise would have been expressed on those occasions when cavalry defeated infantry in line, when they might be ridden down or the flanks rolled up, if the infantry were disordered or caught before they had a chance to form square. The plight of the infantry in such circumstances might be desperate, as William Grattan observed of the charge of Le Marchant's cavalry at Salamanca. As the French infantry endeavoured to form square, 'the motion of the countless bayonets as they clashed together might be likened to a forest about to be assailed by a tempest'; but the cavalry got among them 'before the evolution was half completed ... killing or trampling down all before them. The conflict was severe, and the troopers fell thick and fast; but their long heavy swords cut through bone as well as flesh. The groans of the dying, the cries of the wounded, the roar of the cannon, and the piteous moans of the mangled horses ... was enough to unman men'.[122]

Those who escaped the swinging sabres scrambled away under the horses, and ran to the *British* infantry for protection from the British cavalry, the British infantry perhaps showing some fellow-feeling towards their enemies, knowing the awful fate that could befall broken infantry when assailed by cavalry.

One of the infantry's few chances of salvation under such circumstances was to fall flat or duck low, beneath the reach of the sabres; indeed, it was said that in the very action described above, many of the French who had escaped by this means then rose and fired at the horsemen who had just passed, which caused more casualties than had the initial musketry while the cavalry was approaching. The casualties incurred in such actions could vary dramatically. An example was provided at Austerlitz, when the French 4th Line's 1st Battalion formed square to resist a charge by the Russian Guard Cuirassiers but was then swept by canister fire. One attack was beaten off, but the next rode down the square and captured the battalion's Eagle. The supporting regiment, the 24th Léger, was ridden down in line. The latter's casualties were severe, but the 4th escaped with only eighteen dead. Nevertheless, a regiment which had suffered such trauma might be put out of action for a considerable time, even if casualties had not been heavy; in this particular case, for example, it was reported that fugitives streamed back past Napoleon himself, shouted '*Vive l'Empereur!*' but stopped short of rallying to him, even though the 4th was sufficiently composed to fight on later in the day. Alternatively, stalwart infantry might re-form quickly: for example, at Jena the French 7th

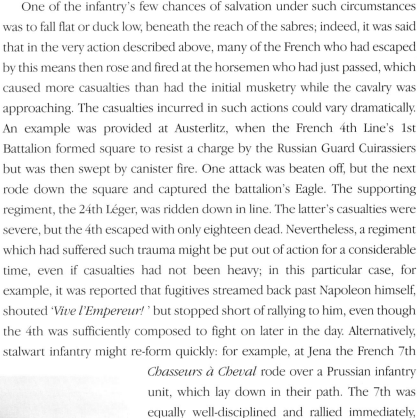

Chasseurs à Cheval rode over a Prussian infantry unit, which lay down in their path. The 7th was equally well-disciplined and rallied immediately, but its commander chose a different way back, riding through a Saxon regiment, as the Prussians originally engaged had stood up and had already re-formed.

Some conception of the sensations of riding through a broken infantry formation were recorded by William Tomkinson:

French 2nd Hussar, c. 1803, showing the suspension of the carbine from the shoulder-belt. This regiment retained its old title, 'Chamborant', unofficially during the imperial period; as shown in a contemporary illustration by its colonel, Jean-François-Thérèse Barbier, the élite company at this period appears to have worn the fur-covered shako or peaked busby shown here. (Print after Rozat de Mandres.)

The enemy's infantry behind the hedge gave us a volley, and being close at them, and the hedge nothing more than some scattered bushes without a ditch, we made a rush and went into their column ... we completely succeeded, many of the infantry immediately throwing down their arms and crowding together for safety. Many too ran away up the next rising ground. We were riding in all directions at parties attempting to make their escape, and in many instances had to cut down men who had taken up their arms after having in the first instance laid them down. From the appearance of the enemy lying together for safety, they were some yards in height, calling out, from the injury of one pressing upon another, and from the horses stamping upon them (on their legs). I had ridden after a man who took up his musket and fired at one of our men, and on his running to his comrades, my horse trod on them. (He had only one eye [Cyclops] and trod the heavier from not seeing them). Lieutenant Beckwith, 16th, stood still and attempted to catch this man on his sword; he missed him, and nearly ran me through the body. I was following the man at a hand gallop.[123]

If unsteady infantry were extremely vulnerable to cavalry, then to a lesser degree the reverse was true. For infantry to charge cavalry was an extremely unusual occurrence under normal circumstances, and could only succeed when the infantry was steady and the cavalry potentially the reverse. Perhaps the most famous example was the attack mounted at Minden (1759) by Spörke's division of six British and three Hanoverian battalions, which advanced through artillery fire and defeated with musketry a large formation of French cavalry in their front; despite his bad dispositions, the French commander (Contades) admitted that he had never imagined that a single line of infantry could break through three lines of cavalry. Another celebrated example occurred at Liegnitz (1760), when the Prussian Bernburg Regiment (assisted by the Prinz Ferdinand Regiment) joined in a cavalry attack against Austrian horse, which they engaged with their bayonets. Just as the Minden attack had not been planned deliberately, so was that of the Bernburg Regiment spontaneous, its men almost out of control in their desire to avenge their earlier disgrace at Dresden. At El Bodon (1811) the British 5th Foot, in line, attacked a force of French dragoons which had just overrun a Portuguese battery, and drove them away, though

French 4th Hussar, c.1805, with carbine drawn and ready to skirmish. Note that the weapon is still hooked to the spring-clip on his belt. (Print after Rozet de Mandres.)

Murat leads the charge at Jena. (Print after H. Chartier.)

again there were exceptional circumstances: had the cavalry not been 'blown' and disordered by their recent charge, the attack could surely not have succeeded. At Borodino the Russian Litovski (Lithuanian) Regiment of the Lifeguard bayonet-charged Nansouty's cavalry, which had already been disordered by musketry from the squares formed by this and other regiments. At La Fère-Champenoise a brigade of French National Guard similarly advanced with the bayonet against enemy cavalry. All these actions involved infantry in steady formations, and cavalry sometimes in considerable disorder.

Another incident emphasises what *could* be achieved under these circumstances. At Quatre Bras two companies of the British 2nd Battalion, 44th Foot under Lieutenant Alexander Riddock had been thrown forward as skirmishers, but had run out of ammunition and consequently were told to retire to their battalion's square. As they did so they were engulfed by a French cavalry charge, which Riddock compared to a swarm of bees; but instead of forming a 'rallying square' to give his men some protection, Riddock assembled them into a four-deep phalanx, the rear ranks with ported arms and the front with levelled bayonets, and charged through the cavalry until they reached safety. That so small a unit could force its way through cavalry – even though it must have been disordered by its charge – demonstrates what was possible, against even the finest cavalry, provided that the infantry kept its nerve.

NOTES

The sources of quotations listed in the footnotes refer to titles which appear in the Bibliography. The following abbreviations are used to identify contemporary publications:

BML : *British Military Library or Journal*
CUSM : *Colburn's United Service Magazine*
USJ :*United Service Journal*
USM : *United Service Magazine*
WD : Wellington, 1st Duke of. *Dispatches of Field Marshal the Duke of Wellington*, ed. J. Gurwood, London 1834–8

1. *USJ*, 1831, vol. II, pp. 205–6.
2. Gleig, p. 163.
3. *USJ*, 1831, vol. II, p. 3; Thersites was an unruly member of the Greek rank-and-file in *The Iliad*.
4. *USM*, 1843, vol. II, p. 433.
5. Stepney, p. 165.
6. *USJ*, 1834, vol. I, p.121.
7. Bismarck, p. 134.
8. *WD*, vol. IX, p. 150.
9. *WD*, vol. X, p. 539.
10.*USJ*, 1836, vol. III, p. 144.
11. Stepney, p. 257.
12. *USM*, 1843, vol. II, p. 292.
13. *CUSM*, 1845, vol. III, pp. 97–8.
14. *USM*, 1843, vol. I, pp. 525–6.
15. *USJ*, 1834, vol. II, p. 453.
16. *CUSM*, 1844, vol. II, p. 439.
17. Maxwell, vol. II, pp. 138–9.
18. *Public Ledger*, 9 March 1813.
19. Rocca, pp. 72–3.
20. Hay, pp. 181–2.
21. *USJ*, 1831, vol. II, p. 60.
22. *WD*, vol. II, pp. 678–9.
23. *Morning Chronicle*, 16 July 1798.
24. De Gonneville, vol. II, p. 100.
25. *USJ*, 1831, vol. II, p. 61.
26. See Brotherton, p. 51.
27. 'New Light on the Flanders Campaign of 1793: Contemporary Letters of Captain J. G. Le Marchant', ed. Lieutenant-Colonel A. H. Burne, in *Journal of the Society for Army Historical Research*, vol. XXX (1952), p. 117.
28. Le Marchant, p. 44.
29. *USJ*, 1831, vol. II, p. 61.
30. *London Gazette*, 15 June 1811.
31. *USJ*, 1840, vol. III, pp. 369–70.
32. Ibid., vol. II, p. 437.
33. Cruso, p. 30.
34. *USJ*, 1831, vol. II, p. 73.
35. Ibid.
36. Dyneley, p. 46.
37. Tomkinson, pp. 115–16.
38. Swabey, p. 114.
39. *USJ*, 1834, vol. II, p. 453.
40. Leeke, pp. 56–7.
41. Marbot, vol. II, pp. 628–9.
42. Mercer, vol. I, pp. 351–2.
43. Brotherton, p. 80.
44. Napoleon, cccvii.
45. The documents are quoted in Strachan (1975), pp. 36–7.
46. For details of the early introduction of cuirasses and helmets, see Elting, pp. 230–1.
47. *Historical Records of the Queen's Own Cameron Highlanders*, compiled by the regimental committee, Edinburgh & London, 1909, vol. I, p. 91.
48. 'Near Observer', pp. 82–3.
49. Cotton, p. 260.
50. Croker, vol. I, p. 330.
51. Mercer, vol. I, p. 345.
52. 'General Hawley's "Chaos"', ed. Revd. P. Sumner, in *Journal of the Society for Army Historical Research*, 1948, vol. XXVI, p. 92.
53. Marbot, vol. I, p. 300.
54. Tomkinson, pp. 152–3.
55. *CUSM*, 1846, vol. I, p. 383.
56. *USJ*, 1831, vol. II, p. 206.
57. *USJ*, 1834, vol. III, p. 399.
58. Leach, pp. 268–9.
59. *USJ*, 1831, vol. II, p. 61.
60. Ibid., p. 69.
61. Ibid., p. 75.
62. Ibid.
63. Ibid., pp. 61, 70.
64. Barrett, vol. I, p. 277.
65. *USM*, 1843, vol. I, p. 578.
66. Tomkinson, p. 135.
67. *USJ*, 1831, vol. II, p. 76.
68. Kincaid, p. 235.
69. R. B. James in Fraser, p. 168.
70. This and succeeding quotation from Wilson, and see also *Royal Military Chronicle*, 1812, pp. 206–7.
71. Austin, pp. 62, 69.
72. R. B. James in Fraser, p. 169.
73. Boutflower, p. 173.
74. Gordon, p. 66.
75. Tomkinson, pp. 98–9.
76. *The Trial of Colonel Quentin*, London 1814, p. 76.
77. Adye, p. 179.
78. Ibid., p. 167.
79. Hay, p. 179.
80. Warnery, pp. 18–19.
81. *Instructions to be Observed for the Formation and Movements of the*

Cavalry, 1799, London, 1801 edn., p. 2. (Henceforth, *Instructions* ...

82. *USJ*, 1831, vol. II, p. 530.

83. *Instructions* ..., pp. 35–6, 39.

84. Ibid., pp. 33–5.

85. *CUSM*, 1844, vol. II, pp. 438–9.

86. Warnery, p. 49.

87. *London Chronicle*, 3 May 1794, p. 420.

88. *USJ*, 1831, vol. II, p. 73.

89. Tomkinson, p. 101.

90. *USM*, 1843, vol. I, p. 190, and in Farmer, vol. II, pp.143–4.

91. *WD*, vol. VII, p. 277 (February 1811).

92. Marbot, vol. II, p. 493.

93. Gordon p. 102.

94. *Instructions* ..., p. 34.

95. *BML*, vol. II, pp. 496–7.

96. Lieutenant Robert Winchester in Siborne, p. 383.

97. De Gonneville, vol. II, p. 31.

98. *The Courier*, 20 April 1811.

99. *Instructions* ..., p. 33.

100. Tomkinson, pp. 135–6.

101. Ibid., p. 153.

102. Gordon, p. 107.

103. Maxwell, vol. II, pp. 138–9.

104. *WD*, vol. IX, p. 240.

105. *CUSM*, 1844, vol. I, p. 439.

106. Alison, vol. V, p. 380; the source of Kellermann's note to this effect is detailed in ibid., p. 383.

107. This translation from Lachouque & Brown, p. 88.

108. *USJ*, 1831, vol. II, p. 526.

109. The story is recounted in Pawly, p. 108.

110. See 'Two Letters of General Horace Churchill', in *Army Quarterly*, July 1935, pp. 292–7.

111. *BMJ*, vol. I, p. 139.

112. *USJ*, 1831, vol. II, p. 13.

113. Ibid.

114. *USJ*, 1834, vol. II, p. 463.

115. *USJ*, 1831, vol. II, p. 74.

116. *CUSM*, 1852, vol. II, p. 525.

117. Mill, Major. J., 'Services in Ireland, the Peninsula, New Orleans and Waterloo', ed. Captain. W. McD. Mill, in *USM*, September, 1870.

118. Tomkinson, p. 280.

119. Ibid., p. 119.

120. *USJ*, 1838, vol. I, p. 208.

121. Hodenberg, C. von, 'A Dragoon of the Legion', ed. Sir Charles Oman, in *Blackwood's Magazine*, March 1913, p. 299.

122. *USJ*, 1834, vol. II, p. 185.

123. Tomkinson, pp. 312–3.

BIBLIOGRAPHY

In addition to the works referred to in the Footnotes, this by no means exhaustive list includes some works of general relevance to the subject of Napoleonic weaponry and warfare.

Adye, R. W. *The Bombardier and Pocket Gunner*, 2nd rev. edn., London, 1802.

Alison, Sir Archibald, Bt. *History of Europe from the Commencement of the French Revolution to the Restoration of the Bourbons*, Edinburgh and London, 1860.

Anon. *Instructions and Regulations for the ormations and Movements of the Cavalry*, London, 1801.

Ardant du Picq, C. J. J. J. *Battle Studies,* trans. J. N. Greely and R. C. Cotton, New York, 1921.

Austin, T. *Old Stick-Leg: Extracts from the Diaries of Major Thomas Austin*, ed. H. H. Austin, London, 1926.

Barrett, C. R. B. *History of the XIII Hussars*, Edinburgh and London, 1911.

Bismarck, F. W. von. *Lectures on the Tactics of Cavalry*, trans. N. L. Beamish, London, 1827.

Blackmore, H. L. *British Military Firearms*, London, 1961.

Boutflower, C. *The Journal of an Army Surgeon during the Peninsular War*, privately published, n.d.

Brack, A. F. de. *Light Cavalry Outposts*, London, 1876.

Brotherton, T. *A Hawk at War*, ed. B. Perrett, Chippenham, 1986.

Chandler, D. C. *The Campaigns of Napoleon*, London, 1967 (leading modern study).

Colin, J. *La Tactique et la Discipline dans les Armées de la Révolution*, Paris, 1902.

Cotton, E. *A Voice from Waterloo*, 9th edn., Brussels, 1900.

Croker, J. W. *Correspondence and Diaries*, London, 1885.

Cruso, J. *Militarie Instructions for the Cavallrie*, Cambridge, 1632.

Dyneley, T. 'Letters written by Lieut General Thomas Dyneley while on Active Service between the Years 1806 and 1815', ed. Colonel. F. A. Whinyates, in *Minutes of the Proceedings of the Royal Artillery Institution*, vol. XXIII, 1896, r/p London, 1984.

Elting, J. R. *Swords around a Throne: Napoleon's Grande Armée*, London, 1988 (very important modern study).

Farmer, C. *The Light Dragoon*, ed. Revd. G. R. Gleig, London, 1844.

Ffoulkes, C., and Hopkinson, E. C. *Sword, Lance and Bayonet*, Cambridge, 1938.

Fraser, E. *Napoleon the Gaoler*, London, 1914.

Gleig, Revd G. R. *The Subaltern*, Edinburgh, 1872.

Glover, M. *Warfare in the Age of Bonaparte*, London, 1980.

Glover, R. *Peninsular Preparation: The Reform of the British Army 1795–1809*, Cambridge, 1963.

Gonneville, A. O. Le H. de. *Recollections of Colonel de Gonneville*, ed. C. M. Yonge, London, 1875.

Gordon, A. *A Cavalry Officer in the Corunna Campaign 1808–1809*, ed. Colonel H. C. Wylly, London, 1913.

Griffith, P. *Forward into Battle: Fighting Tactics from Waterloo to Vietnam*, Chichester, 1981.

— *The Art of War in Revolutionary France 1789–1802*, London, 1998.

— (ed.). *A History of the Peninsular War, vol. IX: Modern Studies of the War in Spain and Portugal 1808–1814*, London. 1999.

— (ed.). *Wellington Commander: The Iron Duke's Generalship*, Chichester, 1985.

Guy, A. J. (ed.). *The Road to Waterloo: The British Army and the Struggle Against Revolutionary and Napoleonic France, 1793–1815,* London, 1990.

Hay, W. *Reminiscences 1808–1815 under Wellington*, ed. Mrs S. C. I. Wood, London, 1901.

Haythornthwaite, P. J. *Weapons and Equipment of the Napoleonic Wars*, Poole, 1979.

— *The Napoleonic Source Book*, London, 1990.

— *The Armies of Wellington*, London, 1994.

Hughes, Major-General B. P. *Firepower: Weapons Effectiveness on the Battlefield 1630–1850*, London, 1974.

Jomini, H. A. de. *The Art of War*, London, 1862.

Kincaid, Sir John. *Adventures in the Rifle Brigade*, London, 1830, and *Random Shots from a Rifleman*, London, 1835, r/p in combined edn., London, 1908.

Lachouque, H., and Brown, A. S. K. *The Anatomy of Glory*, London, 1962 (history of Napoleon's Imperial Guard).

Leach, J. *Rough Sketches in the Life of an Old Soldier*, London, 1831.

Leeke, Revd W. *A Supplement to the History of Lord Seaton's Regiment ... at the Battle of Waterloo*, London, 1871.

Le Marchant, D. *Memoirs of the late General Le Marchant*, London, 1841.

Marbot, J. B. A. M. *The Memoirs of Baron de Marbot*, trans. A. J. Butler, London, 1913.

Maxwell, Sir Herbert. *The Life of Wellington*, London, 1899.

Mercer, General A. C. *Journal of the Waterloo Campaign*, Edinburgh and London, 1870.

Mitchell, Colonel J. *Thoughts on Tactics and Military Organization*, London, 1838.

Nafziger, G. F. *Imperial Bayonets: Tactics of the Napoleonic Battery, Battalion and Brigade as found in Contemporary Regulations*, London and Mechanicsburg, 1996 (important comparison and assessment of the various manoeuvre-regulations).

Napoleon. *New Letters of Napoleon I*, ed. Lady M. Lloyd, New York, 1894.

'Near Observer'. *The Battle of Waterloo ... by a Near Observer*, London, 1816.

Nosworthy, B. *Battle Tactics of Napoleon and his Enemies*, London, 1995 (important modern study).

Oman, Sir Charles. *History of the Peninsular War*, Oxford, 1902–30.

— *Wellington's Army 1808–14*, London, 1912.

Pawly, R. *The Red Lancers*, Marlborough, 1998.

Robson, B. *Swords of the British Army*, London, 1975.

Rocca, A. J. M. de. *Memoirs of the War of the French in Spain*, London, 1815, r/p as *In the Peninsula with a French Hussar*, London, 1990.

Rothenberg, G. E. *Napoleon's Great Adversaries: The Archduke Charles and the Austrian Army 1792–1814*, London, 1982.

— *The Art of War in the Age of Napoleon*, London, 1977.

Siborne, Major-General H. T. (ed.). *The Waterloo Letters*, London, 1891.

Stepney, S. Cowell. *Leaves from the Diary of an Officer of the Guards*, London, 1854.

Strachan, H. *British Military Uniforms 1768–1796*, London, 1975.

— *From Waterloo to Balaklava: Tactics, Technology and the British Army 1815–1854*, Cambridge, 1985 (concerning the military developments which occurred after the Napoleonic Wars, but also the lessons learned in those wars).

Swabey, W. *Diary of Campaigns in the Peninsula*, ed. Colonel F. A. Whinyates, Woolwich, 1895; r/p London, 1984.

Tomkinson, W. *The Diary of a Cavalry Officer in the Peninsula and Waterloo Campaigns*, ed. J. Tomkinson, London, 1895.

Wagner, E. *Cut and Thrust Weapons*, London,1967 (covers many of the regulation patterns of the principal nations).

Warnery, General K. E. von. *Remarks on Cavalry*, London, 1798; r/p with intro. by Brent Nosworthy, London, 1997.

Wilson, Sir Robert. *Brief Remarks on the Character and Composition of the Russian Army*, London, 1810.

Wood, Sir Evelyn. *Achievements of Cavalry*, London,1897.

— *Cavalry in the Waterloo Campaign*, London, 1895.

PERIODICALS

Many periodicals contain material relevant to the subject of Napoleonic tactics and weaponry, including a number devoted exclusively to the Napoleonic period. Many of the more general periodicals also contain articles of relevance, including the journals of learned societies such as the *Carnet de la Sabretache* or the *Journal of the Society for Army Historical Research*, as well as commercial publications such as the British *Military Illustrated* or the French *Uniformes* (ex-*Gazette des Uniformes*) and *Tradition*. Among those concerned with 'minor tactics' was the journal of the New Jersey Association of Wargamers, *Empires, Eagles and Lions*, originally published in Cambridge, Ontario, which presented much contemporary information and discussion.

INDEX